ADVENTURES WITH THE UNIVERSE

H.L. SAVINO

INTRODUCTION

Are you feeling desperate and stuck, broke, one swipe of your bank card away from an overdraft fee?

Do you lie awake at night, wondering how you'll pay your bills? Do you have big dreams but no idea how to make them happen? Worst of all–do you wonder if you're worthy of the beautiful love, wealth, luxury and fabulous life you want?

You can change your life in ninety days. In this book you will learn the "ABCs of abundance", the three step framework that transformed my life and took me from broke to multi-millionaire in six years, from working a job I hated to achieving my lifelong dream of being a bestselling author. To this day, I use the ABCs to turn my mood from desperate to joyful in an instant.

YOU WILL LEARN HOW TO:

- Change your mindset from crushing lack and despair to abundance.
- Float out of the rut you're in—whether you're broke or if you're making money but something's missing.
- Craft your perfect life and remove any mental blocks or beliefs that are stopping you from going after it.
- Build new positive feelings of self-worth so you become magnetic and effortlessly pull in your goals.
- Turn your home into the perfect oasis of luxury that makes you feel like royalty.
- Reframe or remove beliefs that are holding you back, replacing them with new beliefs that help you soar.
- Release your stress, sit back and let the magic happen
- Be happier by choosing yourself.
- Relax and receive all the wealth and success you deserve.
- Believe you deserve it all.

AND MOST OF ALL: Re-imagine your life as an Adventure with the Universe, a glorious journey where you leap and let the magic happen!

Over the next three months, you'll get a new adventure each week, a quest to embark on. The adventures are simple and easy to follow, and you're not going it alone. You have the perfect, all-knowing, all-loving guide to show you the way to abundance. The Universe is Gandalf on steroids, or the genie from Aladdin, but with unlimited power and unlimited wishes. The Universe is here for you, and it can't wait to step in and transform your life.

THIS BOOK CAN HELP you if:

- You're down to your last $106 even though you work all the time.
- You lie awake at night wondering how you'll pay your bills, how it will all work out.
- You want your life to be more than a depressing scramble to stay ahead of overdraft fees.
- You have big goals, big dreams but you don't see a way to make them happen.
- You've always imagined your days unfolding in gorgeous, Pinterest worthy moments. You want to travel to far flung tropical paradises where you eat breakfast in bed and walk the beach with the warm breeze in your hair. Fly first class. Eat fancy cheese! Or just have some dang money so when you're checking out at the grocery store, you're not afraid an extra carton of strawberries will overdraft your account!
- You want more but you're afraid to get started, or maybe you got started but you're stuck back in the grind, exhausted and wondering how to break free.
- You have big dreams but some part of you believes it's not possible for you. You wonder, "Who am I to live a fabulous life? Who am I to be

the wealthiest person I know? Who am I to have millions in my bank account?"

A FEW YEARS AGO, I was in this rut. Smart, hardworking, trying hard to figure things out and feeling like I was failing at every turn. I had negative $106 in my bank account, I lived in a hundred year old house that looked like it was falling over, and I drove a car that had no air conditioning, even though I lived in Central Virginia, where the summer weather averaged ninety-five degree heat and 300% humidity. I was working what was supposed to be my dream job. It turned into a nightmare with an evil boss who made us fly cross country to work weekends and still expected us to be fresh at our desks on Monday. Plus, I had a one hour commute, one way. In a car with no AC.

On my way to work one day, I drove across a bridge. Halfway across, I decided I wanted better for myself. I was working so hard but I was still trapped by my own self doubt, and I was ready to break free.

The problem was that I followed what other people decided should be my life plan. I went to school, graduated and got a job, a house, a car. If I had any desires, any intuition or inkling of what I wanted, I stuffed that down, slammed the door and numbed myself to it.

Maybe you're doing the same thing. You're doing all the things you're supposed to do and buying all the things that are supposed to make you happy. You're trying so hard to make it work, and you're so busy doing all the things that don't work, you're tired and have no energy or time to focus on your desires and dreams.

But there's a part that knows your life can be epic, and it

won't shut up and let you forget. It keeps nudging you onto the right path, over and over. It nudged you to pick up this book.

The Universe is Gandalf on steroids, or the genie from Aladdin, but with unlimited power and unlimited wishes.

It's time to stop living your life for someone else. It's time to stop saying no to your dreams. When I decided to take the leap and choose myself, everything changed. I crossed the bridge to a new life, one that I designed. It took a leap of faith but the Universe was waiting to catch me.

Today I have my dream life. I work for myself and do what I love. My business earns millions and allows me to buy whatever I want, whenever I want–a Tesla X, vacations at St. Regis Bahia beach resort, an apartment for my mom, a gorgeous cashmere sweater to add to my coastal grandma wardrobe.

I went from being broke and desperate and unable to pay my bills to living my dream life. I have a dream career where I work from home. My main business expenses are lattes and yoga pants, and I built a successful online business from $0 to over a million a year in income in six years.

I did this by following the three part framework, the ABCs of abundance, that I will teach to you in this book. Because you deserve to create your dream life too.

These adventures won't feel like work. It'll feel like play. They'll be easier than anything you've ever done, because it's what you are meant to do. Trusting the Universe is like letting yourself exhale after years of holding your breath.

I wrote this book to help you realize your dream life, but also to remind myself of the journey I took from a broke, depressing existence to an abundant life. Because there are days when I forget that my life is a series of Adventures with the Universe. I get grouchy. I drive myself towards my goals, instead of allowing them to arrive on my doorstep. Each chapter in this book contains a new adventure with practical steps to move you from lack to abundance. When I follow the steps, money flows into my bank account like magic.

I want that for you! You deserve money. Not only a swimming pool full of cash, but freedom, wealth, success, satisfaction and happiness. A deep seated contentment that allows you to skip past stress when things go wrong.

When you follow the steps in the following chapters, you'll embark on Adventures with the Universe. And when the Universe gets involved, magic happens. Your life will be transformed:

- You wake up refreshed and excited to start your new day. You sleep well because you're not anxious or worried about bills. You can relax and drink your morning latte from your favorite Mincing Mockingbird mug.
- You swipe your debit card at the grocery store without worrying whether the money is there. The money is there and it will always be there. You're confident that your bank account will have a fresh fount of money to buy all the fancy cheese and strawberries you want.
- Your home is cozy and comfy and looks like a magazine spread. Everywhere you look you see

the books and chairs, framed art and succulent plants you love.
- You're resilient and always seeing new opportunities. Any obstacle in your path is a tiny pebble–easy to step over or kick out of your way.
- You feel good about money. You're relaxed when you pay your bills, and confident when you look at your bank account. The thought of balancing your checkbook doesn't send you spiraling into despair.
- Your work is energizing and uplifting, and you know you're living your life's purpose. You set your own schedule and are able to take plenty of time off for relaxing and vacations.
- You have time and space to create what you want, whether it's creating a new course to help people learn how to train their puppies in twenty days or writing a book of your heart.
- You float along on a cloud of bliss, free and happy, instead of stressed and overwhelmed. You are living your dream life.

ARE you ready to create your best life? Over the next ninety days you're going to go on adventures with the Universe. It's going to be fun and freeing. All you need is your Adventures with the Universe Journal and something to write with, plus this book. Each week has a new adventure for you to embark on with the Universe. Don't worry, it'll be fun and easy. You'll play games with the Universe and do magic spells, and each adventure is crafted to build your trust in the Universe. In your Adventures with the Universe journal, you'll record proof that the Universe is there for you, and waiting to hand you all the wealth and success you deserve. And you do deserve it. You just have to believe and receive it. Once you do that, your life will change so fast you'll wonder if your new life was waiting in the wings to rush in the moment you blinked (it was).

Ask the Universe to deliver, and it will.

IF YOU DON'T THINK you can change, consider this: Every day, three hundred and thirty BILLION cells are replaced in your body. The old cells are recycled and make way for new, vibrant, life-giving cells. Approximately every ninety days, you're a new you. Without any conscious effort, the fabric and reality of you is transformed.

With so much turnover, so much change, it'd take a huge act of self-will NOT to change. That's why moving towards abundance is easy. You're relaxing your resistance and letting go.

It helps if you have an open mind and a belief that your life can change and change for the better, but if you're not quite there yet, it's okay. Come along for the journey and let the Universe do the rest.

OVERVIEW

Over the next three months, you will learn the ABCs of abundance.

A stands for Allow
B stands for Believe
C stands for Clear

WE START with C and go backwards, so I guess it's the CBAs of abundance. Whatever. It's not a linear process, it's a Mobius strip you can cycle through over and over, whether you're broke or already a millionaire.

If you're super stressed right now, dive into Month One and learn the steps to clearing your abundance blocks. Clearing out the clutter will help shift your mood and make space for awesome things to flow into your life.

. . .

Here's the framework we'll follow to learn the ABCs of abundance:

- Month One: Clear. You will learn how to clear any money or abundance blocks holding you back.

- Month Two: Believe. You'll build belief in yourself and your infinite being, your connection to the Universe and the Source energy that makes life possible.

- Month Three: Allow. You will learn to allow abundance and money to flow into your life. By the time you get to month three, you'll understand how easy it is to open up and receive everything you want.

To get started, you'll need a journal and something to write with. Each week you'll read a new chapter and follow the steps to go on the outlined adventure. If you have the Adventures with the Universe Journal, you can use that, but any old journal (or pile of notecards or stone tablet) will do. Each adventure will have its own set of instructions and you can use the whole week to carry them out. Remember, the Universe is your guide and is on call to make things magical.

Your journal will be your adventure log, written proof of all the great things happening to you.

Some adventures are big, others are small. Some adventures will be easy to you and others will challenge you to take a leap of faith. Feel free to half-ass things–do as much of the adventure as you can. You can skip weeks and come back to them later. You can repeat adventures as often as you like–that's what I do! I use these adventures to shift my mood when I'm grouchy and stressed.

By the end of this book, you will understand the truth: your whole life is an Adventure with the Universe. The highs and lows of the rollercoaster can be fun and thrilling – if you'll allow it.

THE MORNING of March 2006 I woke up in a cozy hostel in Trondheim, Norway. It was the last day of my week-long trip and it was time for me to get to the airport and fly to London.

I packed my bags and stepped into the hall, where a horrible sight greeted me. The clock on the wall said it was an hour later than I thought it was. I was officially an hour behind schedule. I was going to miss my flight.

I called the airline and got no answer–it was a Sunday. I went online and tried to switch my flight but weirdly there were no more flights to London available. The next flight available wasn't until Tuesday, which is when I was due to fly from England back to the States. I was a student traveling on a budget and didn't have extra money for missed flights and extra tickets.

Frantic, I called a taxi and begged the driver to take me to the airport as fast as he could. I hoped he would take this opportunity to practice qualifying for the Indy 500. Instead, as we pulled up to the tiny airport, he pointed to the plane angling into the sky and joked, "That's probably your flight."

Inside the airport I passed a group of French football players sitting in a pile of their duffel bags and gear with their heads in their hands. I was not the only one who had missed my flight.

When I got to the counter I was a grouchy mess. In my scramble to try to rebook my flight before I jumped into the taxi, I hadn't taken the time to brush my hair or change out of my pajamas. The lady behind the airline counter must have thought I was nuts, a red-faced college student with bird's nest brown hair and baggy sweats under her big winter coat, snarling and snapping when she told me that the flight was gone.

"Can you get me out on a different flight?" I asked in desperation. She confirmed what I found online: there were no flights to London from this podunk airport until next Tuesday.

At this point, I felt as dejected as the French guys looked. I charged downstairs and locked myself in a bathroom stall. I was all alone in a country where I didn't speak the language. So far, I'd been managing okay, booking train passes, buying *fiskesuppe*, chatting with kind Norwegians in homespun wool sweaters. I'd done a great job of navigating the friendly country. But I was ready to be gone. I had a few hundred dollars in my bank account, no way of calling my London boyfriend to let him know I wasn't going to be waiting at Gatwick for him to pick me up, and no way home.

I hid in the bathroom stall, head in hands. I had scrambled and spun out on a hamster wheel, trying to fix things, and gotten nowhere. I had nothing left to give.

So I asked for help.

I was raised as a Christian and I had a close relationship

with God. Nowadays, I call God "The Universe", but the concept of an all-loving, all-knowing being who cares for me remains the same.

There in the bathroom stall, I spoke frankly. "Hey, God? I've been taught all my life that You are my "Heavenly Father". If that's true, then You know I'm stuck right now. If You really are my Father–and I believe You are–then I need You to take care of this. I need You to fix everything and get me home."

It was a simple ask, or prayer, in a humble place. The podunk airport had a nice bathroom, with red spruce paneling, but it was still a bathroom stall. And I was a mess.

But with that one conversation, I set my intention. I stopped all my effort and scrambling and handed things over to The Universe, completely. I allowed my fate to be in the hands of a Higher Power. I let go.

What followed was nothing short of magical. A peace washed over me. At that moment, I still had no idea how I was going to get to London and back home to the States. But it didn't matter. God was handling it. Maybe I would stay in Trondheim and make some new Norwegian friends. Maybe I'd sleep in a church or work at a hostel to barter for room and board. I had no idea how things would work out, but I was sure they would. It was off my to do list. It wasn't my job to figure anything out. It was my job to relax and believe that anything was possible.

I rose and dressed in proper clothes. I took the time to brush my teeth and comb my hair.

I floated back upstairs, feeling like a new person.

I'd like to think the desk attendant didn't recognize me with the knots out of my hair and a smile on my face. More likely she was surprised that I looked calm and happy, no longer the grouchy version of myself who'd just confronted her.

I propped my arms on the desk and smiled at her.

"Hi," I said. "I missed my flight. I know it was my fault and there's nothing we can do about that, but I really, really need to be back in London. Today, if possible. Is there any way you can find me a flight that will get me to any airport in London?"

I asked with an open heart and open mind, with no attachment to the outcome. If she said she couldn't help me, it would be okay. Everything would be okay. I didn't know how, but I didn't have to know. I just had to trust the Universe.

Within minutes, the nice airline employee had connected me to one of her colleagues at a different airline. I ran back and forth down the long counter, going from one small flight company to the next.

I was happy, smiling, bubbly. The ladies behind the counter were lovely, and between the two airlines they figured out a two leg flight to London. The only catch was I had an eight-hour layover in Bergen, Norway.

They let me make a phone call so I could explain things to my London boyfriend. He was relieved–picking me up later worked out better for his schedule.

Later, when I returned to the States I checked my bank balance and realized the lady at airline #1 had refunded me for the flight I missed, and booked the other two flights with the flight credit. So I only had to pay a minimal amount.

But that wasn't the best part. I didn't know until I left the Bergen airport to spend my layover in town, but Bergen is one of the most beautiful cities in the world. "City of seven mountains", "the heart of the fjords", Bergen sits at the end of a pristine ocean inlet, nestled between fir-covered mountains. The old wharf, Bryggen, is lined with cheerful houses shining like jewels, with their red, white, orange and blue colors reflected in the waters.

I took a bus into town and walked cobbled streets, dipping into a grocery store to buy licorice chocolates and *fiskesuppe*. I carried my meal to one of the many parks, and ate with a view of the serene ocean and city center, in the shadow of a statue of the composer Grieg.

It was one of the best afternoons of my life.

Years later, recounting this story in an Al-anon meeting, I cried, not because the memory wasn't happy, but because I constantly forget how easy things can be. I waste so much time stressed out and staggering under the weight of the day, when I could simply relax, let go, and let The Universe do all the heavy lifting.

And so can you.

Are you stressed like I was that spring morning? Are you spinning on the hamster wheel, working a hundred times harder to make sure things turn out okay? Are you afraid everything won't work out?

Life can be easy. Relax, and let go. The Universe is waiting to catch you.

LET'S GET STARTED. In your Adventures with the Universe journal, write the following intention. Pretend you're broke and desperate in a bathroom in Trondheim, Norway, and invite the Universe (God, Source Energy, Collective Consciousness) to step in and transform your life.

Use the statement below and modify it to make it yours, or make up your own.

. . .

INTENTION: *I am now open to receiving all the good the Universe wants to send me. I allow abundance to flow in and change every part of my life for the better. Universe, please guide me on this adventure called life. Make it magical! I am relaxed and ready to receive.*

Life can be easy. Relax, and let go. The Universe is waiting to catch you.

INVITATION

Join the Adventures with the Universe Course to explore these Adventures more deeply.

MONTH ONE: CLEAR

"The more grateful I am, the more beauty I see."
  – Mary Davis

In this month we're going to work on clearing any money or abundance blocks holding you back.

Here are the four main categories of abundance blocks:

- The "I'm not worthy/not good enough" block
- The "Money is evil" block
- The "There's not enough to go around" block
- The "More money and success isn't safe" block

CLICK HERE to complete the simple quiz at www.adventureswiththeUniverse.com/quiz to find out what sort of money blocks you have. Then come back here and keep reading. The next few weeks' adventures will help you remove these money blocks and lighten your mental load. You'll feel better instantly.

As you journey through this book, you are going to get comfortable turning your problems over to the Universe. You can do it at any time, and the results are magical.

ADVENTURE ONE

"In a quantum Universe, magic is not the exception but the rule."
—*Arjuna Ardagh*

The Magic Spell

WE'RE GOING to start with a magic spell: a simple and fun adventure that will unlock great things.

The Magic Spell has three steps. The first step is called the Gratitude Game. The second is called the Love list. By the time you're done with the first two steps, you'll be flying high on good feelings. Once you're feeling amazing, you complete step three and make a list of requests to the Universe. Finally, you turn your requests over to the Universe and release your white-knuckle grip on how abundance will come into your life.

I went on this adventure yesterday when my husband took my two kids to the park and I had a quiet moment to myself. I didn't do the Magic Spell completely–I half-assed it. (Remember I said you could half-ass things? I meant it.) After I followed steps one and two, I felt all floaty and happy. For the final steps of the spell, I asked for more business income and visualized earning over three hundred thousand this month. Then I closed my journal and went about my day.

A few hours later, I got a nudge to make a single post in three separate author forums I'm in and let people know my Seven Figure Author course price was increasing. Sales poured in: $10,400 worth in less than 24 hours. $10,000 per day is $300,000 for the month. This happened within hours of my request, and it wasn't hard. It felt like magic.

Turn the page and follow along to unleash some magic into your life.

THE MAGIC SPELL:

YOU WILL NEED:

- A journal and something to write with
- Note cards or extra paper
- A box to keep notes in

STEPS TO CAST THE SPELL:

. . .

Step One: The Gratitude Game

The fastest way to shift your frequency from scarcity to abundance is to focus on what you already have and feel thankful.

How to play:

Write in your journal, "I'm so grateful for _____ because _____." Fill in the first blank with something you're grateful for that's nearby.

Example: "I'm so grateful for my *green couch*."

For the second blank, think of all the reasons why you're grateful for whatever you wrote in the first blank. There are probably tons of reasons, you've just never focused on them.

Example: "I'm so grateful for my green couch *because* I love the color. It looks nice in my living room. Plus, it's comfortable. I've wanted a couch like this ever since I saw the one my mom bought, and then a friend was getting rid of hers for $125! This couch is beautiful, durable, *and* cost me only $125. Win! Thank you, Universe!"

. . .

THIS EXAMPLE IS A BIT MUCH. Most days I don't write a whole soliloquy for this exercise. But I do think those thoughts and, more importantly, *feel* those *feelings.*

If you don't want to write down all of the reasons you're grateful, you can just write down one. But think through all the reasons and feel the feelings of gratitude well up within you. That's the most important part of this game—feeling the feelings. Those feelings make you feel abundant.

I'll say it again, feeling those feelings is the *most* important part of this game. Let's take it a step further. Close your eyes and think of what you just wrote. Feel the feelings of being truly grateful. In *The Magic*, a book on gratitude by Rhonda Byrne that I highly recommend, she encourages you to "say the magic words" three times while feeling these feelings. *"Thank you, thank you, thank you."* You can repeat the words silently. Every time you say "thank you," imagine the feeling getting more intense and swelling to fill your whole body.

Depending on how grouchy I am, it takes me a minute or two to dust off the layer of mucky feelings to get to a place of peace and joy. If you don't feel grateful right away, it's okay. Each time you reach for the feeling of thankfulness and let it wash over you, you're clearing off another layer of grime and grumpiness to get to the relaxed, positive feelings. After you've played this game, you will feel a ton better.

Research supports this finding. Studies show writing in a Gratitude Journal can improve mental health and your relationships with others. There's evidence that you can practice activating a region of your brain called the cingulate cortex and stimulate feelings of gratitude. Gratitude can reduce feelings of cynicism and train your brain to more easily reach for positive memories. Practicing the feelings of love and gratitude creates new pathways in your brain and allows you to focus more on what's wonderful about your life.

In one study, students wrote out a daily gratitude list for fourteen days. According to their trial: *"The gratitude intervention managed to increase positive affect, subjective happiness and life satisfaction, and reduce negative affect and depression symptoms."* These results can last for months.

If you want scientific proof of the power of gratitude, check out these studies:

Wong Y J, et al. Does Gratitude Writing Improve the Mental Health of psychotherapy clients?

Bartlett M, Condon P, et al. Gratitude: prompting behaviors that build relationships

Yu H. Gao X, et al. Decomposing Gratitude: Representation and Integration of Cognitive Antecedents of Gratitude in the Brain

Lúzie Fofonka Cunha, et al. Positive Psychology and Gratitude Interventions: A Randomized Clinical Trial

Philip Watkins: Thieves of Thankfulness: Traits that inhibit gratitude

Philip Watkins: Grateful recounting enhances subjective well-being: The importance of grateful processing

P. Kini, et al. The effects of gratitude expression on neural activity

You can be confident the Gratitude Game can improve your mood and your life.

Write out ten more things you're grateful for, following the same steps as above. After you write the list, reread it and dwell on the FEELINGS of gratitude. Close your eyes and amplify the grateful sensations welling up inside you. Focus on those feelings. Memorize them. Juice the good feelings, marinate in them, let them saturate your whole body and mind.

For more help and inspiration for your gratitude list, check out the prompts in your Adventures in the Universe journal.

Step two: The Love List

This game is designed to get you feeling good as quickly as possible.

How to play:

In your journal, write out a list of 10 things you love most about your life. Write until you have a big smile on your face.

Here are some prompts:

- What do you love about your life?
- Who are the people you love most? What do you love about them?
- What do you love most about the places you've lived?
- What do you love most about nature? The outdoors?
- What do you love most about your body? From the top of your head to the tips of your toes, and all the organs in between.
- What are your favorite foods?
- What are your favorite types of clothes?
- What are your favorite places to visit?
- What are your favorite types of music? What are your favorite songs?

- What are your favorite books, movies, TV shows, video or board or card games, plays, spectacles, things to do on a Friday night?

Once you've filled a page or five, tune in to your feelings. Do you feel good? Amplify that feeling. Dwell in it, if only for a few seconds. Stretch it out as long as you can. Feeling the feelings is the most important part of this step.

Reread your list and let the feelings of love and joy fill your heart. Intensify the feelings. Can you make those good feelings 10x stronger? 100x? 1000x?

For more help and inspiration for your love list, see the prompts in your Adventures with the Universe Journal.

Step three: Describe your Desires.

How to Play:

In your Adventures with the Universe Journal, write down something you want to manifest. It can be big or small. You can write a whole "Want List" (like you'll do in Month Two, Adventure Five) or simply write down the first thing that comes to mind. There's no way to do this wrong. If you're having trouble thinking up what you want, ask the Universe to help you come up with something fun.

Here are a few prompts:

Clothes you want to wear
Foods you want to eat
Gorgeous and fun stuff you want to own
Items, big and small, you want to buy
Places you want to travel
People you want to meet
Experiences you want to have

Step Four: Release your Request

How to Play:

Now that you have a written list of something(s) you want, it's time for the final part of The Magic Spell. For this step, you'll need a box or container of some sort. I have a pretty one I ordered on Etsy inscribed with the words "Ask." I call it my 'Ask box'. But a sturdy shoebox works too.

Take your written request and fold it up and place it in your 'Ask box'. If I've listed out several things, I like to copy each entry separately onto note cards or nice stationery, then fold them up and put them in the box. This is a physical ritual to demonstrate to yourself that you are turning your wants and desires over to the Universe.

Once your request is in the box, it is no longer your responsibility. You've set the intention and it's the job of the Universe to do the rest. Relax. Everything you want is off your to do list. It's now the job of the Universe to deliver your requests in the best and most brilliant way possible. Prepare to be awed!!!!!

ADVENTURE TWO

"...Be transformed by the renewing of your mind." – Paul the Apostle, Letter to the Romans

Remember those money blocks you uncovered in the quiz at www.adventureswiththeUniverse.com/quiz? If you haven't taken it, do it now! Then return here to go on this adventure and learn how to clear those blocks.

Let's review this sample list of abundance blocks. In your journal, you can circle and take notes on the ones you have.

The "I'm not worthy/not good enough" block

Highlight or circle the statements that resonate with you:

- I'm not worthy of earning lots of money.

- I'm not good enough to earn lots of money.
- I don't know enough to get started.
- I don't have anything to offer, I'm not smart or educated or important enough to be successful.
- I'm not ready. I need to know more before I can start.
- My course, product, book, art, or creation isn't ready. I need to add more/fix it/perfect it before it can go out into the world.
- There will never be enough money in my life. I can never earn enough, so why try?
- I'm doing/going to do it wrong. I'm not doing the right things.
- I'm going to mess up. I always mess up and make mistakes, so it's useless to try.
- Other people are better than me.
- I'm a failure. I don't fit in with successful people; I'm not like them.
- People don't like me no matter what I do. People don't want me or what I have to offer.
- I'm a victim, I'm unloved, I'm unlovable, I'm broken.
- I've been cheated/will be cheated again, so it's useless to try.
- I'm too much, I'm overwhelming, I shine too bright, I talk too much, I'm too over-the-top and weird, I'm too smart and being the smartest kid in class isn't safe.
- I've had money and lost it, I suck, I don't deserve more.
- I can't earn money because I'm not a man, I'm queer, I'm not white, I'm not American, I don't speak English as a first language, I don't look or

talk or think like the rich people I know or see on TV.
- Other people deserve money and success, but not me.
- When I do have success, I minimize or apologize for it. I deflect compliments and qualify my success. I still don't know what I'm doing. I earned $100,000 but I spent so much on marketing.
- I'm successful now but it's just a fluke.
- I have to work hard to earn money, otherwise I don't deserve it.
- I'm not worthy if I'm not grinding it out, working 24/7, sleeping as little as possible. I don't deserve to have money flow to me easily and effortlessly. Earning lots of money has to be a struggle.

If you felt any of these statements were true, you have the "I'm not worthy/not good enough" block.

TRUTH: Your self-image is constricted and keeping you small. You think you have to be more–more educated, more skilled, more beautiful, more organized, more put-together, more hard working, older, thinner, healthier, younger, smarter, faster, hungrier... the list goes on and on!

You are worthy as you are. You deserve money now. Once you clear this block you'll see yourself as someone worthy of all the riches you could ever want.

The "Money is evil" block

Highlight or circle the statements that resonate with you:

- Money corrupts people.
- Rich people are evil.
- Being poor means I'm holy/more spiritual/closer to God.
- Poverty is noble.
- Money is the root of all evil.
- If I have more money, I won't be a good person.
- Money is dirty–i.e., physical bills and coins are unclean, and taint my conception of money as a whole.
- The only way to get more money is to scam someone or embrace unethical practices. I don't want to compromise my ethics, so I can only earn a limited amount. Any more than that means I'm a bad person.
- Earning money doing what I love–writing books, creating art or beautiful products, teaching, coaching or serving people–is selling out.
- I love helping people, but if I charge money for it, I'm hurting the people I want to help.
- People in my profession should be poor. Artists should starve. Teachers shouldn't be able to pay their bills. Otherwise they're not doing all they can to serve humanity.
- It's wrong to have more than what I need.

- Life is meant to be hard and test my perseverance. Ease and joy mean I'm not growing spiritually.
- To truly live my calling, I have to be a martyr.

IF YOU FELT any of these statements were true, you have the "Money is evil" block.

TRUTH: abundance is divine. Money isn't evil, it's a tool like a hammer. You can use it for good or otherwise. Rich people are just people. Having more money doesn't make you better than anyone else, and neither does being poor.

I grew up learning "The love of money is the root of all evil", and when I asked a Bible teacher for more clarification, they explained the term "love of money" was called "Mammon", which means "greed." Greed comes from a feeling of lack, a grasping needy sense that there can 'never be enough.' The opposite of greed is unlimited abundance. "You can't serve God and Mammon" makes sense because God is abundance, and Mammon is the opposite of abundance.

You deserve to have all you want or need, regardless of your profession. You can earn money by serving others. And when you embrace abundance, you're helping others even more. It's healthy for people to pay for goods or services that delight them. Release these lies to allow more money into your life.

The "There's not enough to go around" block

Highlight or circle the statements that resonate with you:

- There's a limited amount of money/abundance and if I get more, I'm taking from others.
- There's not enough money, health, water, air, happiness, caviar or land to go around.
- Wanting more is selfish.
- It's okay to want things, but not too much, because then I'm stealing from others. I deserve a little bit but not more.
- There's no such thing as unlimited abundance.
- I can't have it all.
- I can't afford that.
- I have to save every penny.
- No matter what I do, I can't get ahead.
- I'll always be in debt.
- I can only earn money one way.
- I can only earn money working a job. I can't do what I love and earn millions.
- Not everyone can be a millionaire.
- Money doesn't grow on trees–even though it is literally paper, and where do you think paper comes from, Dad?
- There's a limited number of customers/clients and one day I'll run out of people to sell to and my business will have to close.

- I can make a bunch of money but then a karmic rubber band will snap and I'll be hurled back into debt.

IF YOU FELT any of these statements were true, you have the "There's not enough to go around" block.

TRUTH: the Universe and abundance have no limits! When we create from a place of unlimited potential, we unlock more riches for everyone. You're not taking a bigger slice of the pie–you're growing the size of the whole pie! Think of the inventions that make everyone's lives better–from surgeries to solar panels, Shakespeare's plays and Beethoven's symphonies and Botticelli's paintings. These inventions and creations inspire the next wave of inventions and art like the internet and AI, N.K Jemisin's novels and Tracy Chapman's albums.

Choosing abundance over scarcity is a science-backed choice.

For more evidence that abundance is unlimited, look no further than the Simon Abundance Index, a project that tracks commodities and prices. Turns out, over time, commodities get cheaper–or replaced by other resources. The index is named for the economist Julian Simon after his famous bet with biologist Paul Ehrlich. With his wife, Anne, Ehrlich wrote a bestseller called "The Population Bomb" filled with dire predictions of global collapse and mass starvation caused by too many people on the planet. Talk about a scarcity mindset!

Julian Simon had a different view. He wrote a book called "The Ultimate Resource" and predicted that costs for energy and natural resources would plummet and we'd be able to produce plenty of food to support the growing population. In the wager with Paul Ehrlich, Simon bet that the overall price of five metals would decline over a decade. And he won!

The Simon Abundance Index continues to prove that, despite fluctuations in commodity pricing, overall, costs are going down. Either we need less of certain resources, or we find ways to replace them, or we find more efficient ways to produce them. It's important that we conserve and care for our beautiful planet, but more people on the planet means more innovation, more people creating and inventing easier ways to achieve an awesome quality of life.

Choosing abundance over scarcity is a science-backed choice.

Money is like air or water. It flows. That's why it's called 'currency': it moves like a current through many people's hands. Even money I have pooled in my savings account is invested–I've given it to business owners around the world in hopes they grow their business and so grow my retirement stash!

We don't say "I've been healthy most of my life. It's time to give my health up to some sick people." No! Your health doesn't take away from anyone else. In fact, when I'm healthy, I'm better able to care for members of my family who are sick. The more time and effort I invest in my health, the more energy and ideas I have to give others. And my example models higher standards for my kids.

The same goes for money. You having money doesn't

take away from anyone else's ability to have and make money. First of all, you make money by offering value to others. More value in the world blesses everyone! And your example and standards help raise the bar for everyone who knows you.

If you feel like earning more money will put a target on your back, read on to learn about the next abundance block. Don't worry, you'll learn ways to disintegrate all these blocks soon!

The "More money and success isn't safe" block

Highlight or circle the statements that resonate with you:

- If I earn more money, I'll become a target. People will come out of the woodwork to ask for a handout. My family will guilt me into financing their lifestyle. I'll never have any peace!
- I'll be persecuted and made an example of if I get too wealthy/too successful. People will criticize me publicly.
- If I'm more successful and more visible, there will be so much pressure. I can never make a mistake.
- Change is scary, big numbers are scary, the only way I'll be safe is if things stay the same.
- It's scary to have large amounts in my checking or savings account. I'm not sure if I can handle it.
- I'm not good with money.
- I have to save every penny. Disaster and bankruptcy is right around the corner. At any minute, I could lose it all.

- Easy come, easy go.
- If I earn more money, I'll have to pay more in taxes, so I better limit my earnings to only pay the amount of taxes I'm familiar and comfortable with.
- The money will come but then I'll lose it right away, and it will devastate me. It's better to avoid disappointment and not even try.
- I can't get more customers/clients/sell more because then I'll have more refunds/complaints/negative reviews.
- If I sell to people, they'll think I'm using them.
- If I hire people, they'll hate me because I'm the boss.
- Employees/renters/customers are always out to cheat me. They want a handout, they're not willing to pay.
- It's not safe for me to stand out or shine. It is dangerous for me to be myself or be too different or make more money than the richest person I know.
- If I put myself out there to sell something or be successful, I'll look like a fool. People will judge me. I'll be publicly humiliated.
- If I make more money than my friends and family, they'll feel bad. My success will make them feel like a failure and they'll be sad or angry, they will shun, reject and abandon me.
- I can't make more money than my parents, mentor or the most successful person I know. It would be disrespectful.
- It's better to be nice than successful. I can't be both.

- I can't handle more money–I have bad money habits and more money will only lead to disaster. How will I manage it all?
- The thought of having a lot of money in my bank account is intimidating.
- If I shine too bright or work too hard, I'll burn out.
- I've never been successful or earned a lot of money before and it feels scary.
- I tell myself, "I don't know what to do next. I don't know how to make more money." because it's easier to stop myself from thinking up ways to make more money than face my fears.

IF YOU FELT any of these statements were true, then you have the "More money and success isn't safe" block.

TRUTH: Fear holds you back, because it's trying to keep you safe. Your brain wants you to stay in your comfort zone where things are familiar. In primal times, that meant staying close to your campfire and cave, and not venturing out into the forest where a saber tooth tiger might eat you. The unknown is scary, and the fear wants to keep you in a tight, confined space.

In the months to come, you will make wealth and success more familiar. You will normalize having bigger and bigger numbers in your bank account. What was once unknown and scary will become old hat. I used to think having over $1000 in my bank account was a big deal. Now I have tens of thousands of dollars in my business bank account–and if it dips, I make money moves and decisions to top it up to the proper amount. In the following chapters, I'll cover the exact methods I used to 10x my funds. Don't worry, earning and having more money can be easy and effortless.

Follow the steps of each adventure and normalize larger and larger amounts of money. Soon, you will know the truth: you don't need the fear. You are safe in the arms of the Universe.

Are you ready to exhume your money blocks and set them on fire?

Whew, that was a lot! Are you ready to clear some blocks? If your gut is churning and your chest is tight, it's okay. When you follow the next steps to remove these money blocks, it'll lighten your mental, emotional and spiritual load. You'll feel better instantly.

REPEAT AFTER ME:

"I now clear anything that's blocking the flow of money into my life."

REPEAT this statement until you feel lighter. Then, go and do something that feels good. Take a walk or a nap or a relaxing bath. I like to take a shower and repeat the statement and imagine all my old beliefs washing away.

You accepted these beliefs, you put them in place to keep

you safe. You are an infinite, powerful being and you can banish these beliefs with a word or a thought.

If you want more help clearing your abundance blocks, join me and my friend Renee Rose in the Money Magic Membership course. We have regular calls to energetically clear abundance blocks.

Let's try something. I'm going to make a statement, and you're going to get still and pay attention to how it makes you feel.

> Money comes easily and effortlessly.

Okay, now, how do you feel? Repeat the statement in your head. Does it feel light and easy? Or is there a part of you that immediately rejects it? When you start to pay attention, you might hear a rebuttal. I call this the "negative echo."

When I got quiet and listened, I realized every time I spoke positively about money, my brain resisted in the form of a negative echo. That resistance was what I truly believed, and that belief was blocking money from flowing into my life.

> Here are a few examples of the negative echo:
>
> Money comes easily and effortlessly.
>
> <negative echo> "No, it doesn't."

Money comes easily and effortlessly.

<negative echo> "Maybe if you're a crook!"

Money comes easily and effortlessly.

<negative echo> "Easy come, easy go."

YOU MIGHT HEAR something different in rebuttal, but pay attention. If it's negative, it's a money block. If it feels heavy or icky, it's resistance to abundance. Resistance is something you create because you feel unworthy of what you want. It's a sign you have a money block that you put in place to hold yourself back. No one's stopping you but yourself.

My money blocks made my chest ache. Those feelings were blocking me from the money and success I craved. As I cleared them, I moved towards my goals and dreams effortlessly: becoming an author and then a USA today bestselling author writing the books of my heart, getting my work translated into four languages, doing author signings in the US, France, Italy and Scotland, growing a six and then seven figure business that retired my husband and allows us to eat sushi whenever we want.

Now it's your turn to clear your money blocks. Ready for some relief?

First, congratulate yourself for figuring out what you're feeling. For listening to yourself and being aware of the ways you're resisting the flow of money into your life. This is deep work.

Next, thank the feeling. These negative feelings are trying to protect you. You've had some bad experiences with money, some trauma, and your brain has built up a block to money, like a thick wall to protect you from danger. So, even swamped in these negative feelings, take a second to be grateful. Your brain has your back. You're on your own side.

Those blocks were trying to protect you. But you don't need them anymore, so we're going to clear them.

The adventures in the coming weeks are designed to clear money blocks. But for fast relief now, say to yourself:

"I now clear anything that's blocking the flow of money into my life."

I USED to stand in the shower, call up my feelings about money, bills, and my guilt over my money mistakes and clear them one by one. "I clear my bills. I clear my guilt about missing my mortgage payment." I'd pretend the water was washing my money blocks away.

You can clear your beliefs over and over. Let's do it now! I'm going to make a statement about money, and you're going to hear the negative echo and clear it. Do this as many times as it takes to feel relief.

Money comes easily and effortlessly.

<negative echo>

"I clear that belief about money."

Money is good.

<negative echo>

"I clear that belief about money."

I can have all the money I want. Every day it flows into my life.

<negative echo>

"I clear that belief about money."

I love money.

<negative echo>

"I clear that belief, and any other belief that's blocking the flow of money into my life."

I can have what I want.

<negative echo>

"I clear that belief, and any other belief that's blocking the flow of money into my life."

I can afford it.

<negative echo>

"I clear that belief, and any other belief that's blocking the flow of money into my life."

. . .

Did you clear all the resistance that came up when you read those statements? If you're overwhelmed, you might put this book down, and try again later this week. You might have a lot of crud to clear.

If you feel the relief, enjoy the feeling. Be grateful for it. And relax knowing from now on, when negative feelings about money arrive, you can quickly clear them.

Over the next few weeks, you're going to learn many ways to clear your money blocks. Some will work for your situation better than others. But we've been doing a lot of work here, so give yourself a hug and go do something to pamper yourself.

Bonus question to journal about: "What other blocks do I have and how do they stop me?" Ask the Universe to give you the answer and help you clear the blocks away.

ADVENTURE THREE

"The first step in crafting the life you want is to get rid of everything you don't."
— Joshua Becker

What would your home look like if you were wealthy? Would you still have that vase you hate but you're afraid to give away because your aunt gave it to you and you don't want to hurt her feelings? Would you still have the table with the broken leg, the one you keep because it's "good enough"? Would you keep that ugly rug with the stain on it or would you upgrade to one you love that's easier to clean? Would you invest in weekly house cleaning or would you tell yourself "I can't afford it"...even though having your house cleaned would make you feel wealthy and wonderful?

We're meant to live in beautiful spaces, surrounded by people and items we love. Instead, we:

- Hold onto broken items because we tell ourselves we can't afford an upgrade.
- Keep items we hate because someone gave it to us, and we feel unworthy of being surrounded by gorgeous furniture, art and decor we love.
- Let junk pile up, telling ourselves that it's wasteful to throw anything away.
- Hang on to duplicate items or things we don't really need, telling ourselves that one day we might need them.
- Force ourselves to do cleaning tasks we hate, because we were taught getting help is lazy.

Did you spot the money blocks in the bullet points above? Releasing things you don't love is a great way to reinforce new money beliefs.

When we clear the clutter and upgrade our lifestyle, we communicate the following truths to our subconscious:

- "I can't afford to upgrade" becomes "I can afford the beautiful things I love. I deserve them."
- "I have to keep items I hate" becomes "I deserve to be surrounded by things I love. It's safe for me to have my own tastes and preferences. Gently rejecting other people's stuff doesn't mean I reject the people I love."
- "I deserve a clean and cozy space to live in."
- "I can afford to buy what I need, when I need it. I don't need to hang on to items "just in case" because the Universe will provide the money to

buy what I need–or the item I need–at the perfect time."
- Allow ourselves to hire people to clean our bathrooms, make our meals, do our laundry, mow our yards because "We deserve all the help and support we need or desire" and "Life can be easy. I don't have to work hard to prove anything. I'm enough as I am."

THE ACT of clearing out our living space is a powerful way to release our money blocks. One friend cleared out her garage and found a painting she did in elementary school. Holding the canvas, she remembered how her teacher criticized the art she made. It was the first time she felt shame over something she created. She was able to clear the feelings of inadequacy—and her block against earning money from her art melted away.

Another friend went through a divorce and considered downsizing into a rental house. Instead, she chose to use her savings to purchase a large home with a stunning view of the Catalina mountains, a house that made her feel rich. Within two years, she'd doubled her income into the millions, then doubled it again.

In the last adventure, you started clearing away your negative thoughts, emotions and beliefs about money. In this adventure, you'll go a step further and clear the physical clutter–the stuff you're holding on to that's reinforcing your feelings of unworthiness. Our negative beliefs can manifest as junk and trash cluttering up our homes. Our outer world reflects our inner world. Clean up the outer world, and our inner world shifts magically.

Try it now!

~

Clear the Clutter

"Outer order contributes to inner calm." -Gretchen Rubin

STEP ONE: Make a list of things you're grateful for until you're feeling awesome. Focus on the awesome feelings, juice them and amplify them as much as possible.

STEP TWO: Once you're feeling good, imagine or visualize your home as you like it. Dwell on a sense of calm and peace, clean and easy to navigate, everywhere you look is something you love! Invite the Universe to help you design the perfect space in your mind, and connect you with the feelings of freedom, peace and wealth.

STEP THREE: Clear the clutter in your purse or wallet.

If you were a millionaire, what sort of bag would you carry? Upgrade the wallet or purse you're carrying to a beautiful one that makes you feel good.

Start with your wallet or purse. Empty it out. Throw the trash away. Make room for all the money you want to receive.

Take it a step further and upgrade the wallet or purse you're carrying to a beautiful one that makes you feel good. If you were a millionaire, what sort of bag would you carry? A Louis Vuitton Neverfull or a turquoise Kate Spade purse that looks like a typewriter? Or If you have resistance to upgrading, clear it away by repeating "I clear my feelings about deserving nice things."

Step four: Clear the clutter out of your home.

What would it be like to live in a gorgeous home surrounded by art and decor and people you love? What would it feel like?

For me, it means upgrading from dingy carpet to hardwood floors and wool rugs with a modern pattern that hides dirt my kids track in. I have brand new dressers and hygge decor but also a quilt my great-aunt knit for me when I was a baby, and the worn but beautiful wood bed and wardrobe my grandma passed down to me. You decide what you love and want to keep, and guess what? You can always change your mind.

Get three containers or bags. One for trash, one for storage, the other for donating. Go through your house and clean the clutter. Trash goes into the trash. Broken

Adventures with the Universe

and stained items are trash. Most items you haven't used for over a year are either trash or should be donated. If you cannot bring yourself to trash or give away an item, but you are done with it, put it into storage. In a few months, return to the storage box and see if you can let it go.

To paraphrase Barbara Hemphill, "clutter is just [delayed] decisions." Give yourself permission to make the decisions of what to do with all your stuff–to love it or to let it go.

This isn't a mundane chore. Our physical world reflects our mental world, and there are blocks you'll easily banish simply by taking a deep breath and donating all the stuff you've been holding on to "in case you need it someday."

Clear out the old and make way for the new. The Universe abhors a vacuum, which means if you make space for good things in your life, they will come!

Imagine you're moving into your dream home. What would you take with you? Start to distill your stuff down to only those things.

Your goal is to surround yourself with things you love. When you walk into your house and the first thing you see is a vase you hate, it drags down your energy. So give yourself permission to trash or donate that vase, even if it was an heirloom or a gift. If you need extra help with this, I recommend Marie Kondo's method. I also like the Minimalist's philosophy.

Don't be afraid to get rid of things you don't like before you've bought something new. You're making space for the new things you want, and you'll pull them in faster than if you still had the old item lying around.

If you need help with this, hire a cleaning service, or

barter with a friend for their help. Clean up as much as you can and let them help you with the rest.

It's okay to take this in stages. I have toddlers, so I have a houseful of crumbs and puzzle pieces. When things are cluttered, my brain gets itchy. I have a cleaning service come through weekly, and my mental state is so much calmer and at peace when my home is in order.

It's hard after the holiday season, when the entire house is overflowing with my kids' Christmas haul. They're the only two grandchildren, and both sets of grandparents buy out the store. How many stuffed turtles do a four-year-old and six-year-old need? Enough to carpet their bedroom floor.

Wading through the Squishmallows™ yesterday, I asked the Universe for help. "Please clean and declutter my house for me." I sat down and did the Magic Spell in Adventure One, and kept a log of all the magic that followed:

- My husband's friends came over to visit and randomly decided to fix a drawer that'd been broken for months. They pulled out twenty years worth of junk that'd fallen behind it and then they tried to vacuum.
- The vacuum didn't work, so they took that apart and de-linted it, and finished vacuuming.
- Overcome with gratitude, I offered them an electric kettle and Instant Pot™ I'd never used. They hauled those away.

I NOW HAVE a clean kitchen and decluttered pantry, a junk drawer that's been de-junked and now closes completely. Plus a vacuum that works. And it's only been a day! Thank you, Universe.

If you're overwhelmed, ask the Universe to help. The Universe can step in and send you antiquers who want to take your old furniture and knick knacks off your hands, handy people who will fix the sputtering lightbulb in your basement and paint your living room, organization and decorating services that will declutter and style your pantry and linen closet until it's Pinterest worthy! Ask the Universe to make this decluttering process quick and painless, and follow the nudges to let things go.

ASK YOURSELF, "What would it take for me to love the space I'm in?"

A NOTE ON RENTING: my friend Lilian rents a furnished apartment and felt stuck with the decor and layout. But as she grew in income and feelings of deservingness, she realized she could ask the landlord to take away a couch she hated. Lilian writes, "We were able to get a new couch and rug and now the place feels much better. Same with new blackout curtains instead of their shitty blinds, and a bunch of small maintenance fixes. Sometimes a block with renting is "I don't want to fix it/spend money on it because it isn't mine" but for now it IS mine. It's so freeing to just ask the landlord and make changes (or spending a small amount of money on a maintenance issue that they would leave for ages) instead of hating things about our home and feeling powerless."

Ask yourself, "What would it take for me to love the space I'm in?" And follow the nudges to declutter and upgrade and ultimately unlock new feelings of worthiness.

Decluttering uncovers money blocks, so pay attention to what you're feeling. If there's a bunch of junk you're holding on to because "it was expensive and I might want it later and won't be able to afford it," that's a good reason to let it go. Letting go of stuff tells the Universe you're confident you'll be able to afford what you need. And that is the state of abundance.

STEP FIVE: Clear the Digital Clutter. Free up even more mental space so you can focus on the positive instead of getting inundated with the negative. Just as your diet affects your nutrition, your digital diet–what you consume via TV, mail, email, radio and social media–affects your mental health.

TO CLEAR THE DIGITAL CLUTTER:

- TV and radio: Turn off your TV. Turn off the radio. Decide what you want to listen to, and monitor how you feel. Do you feel good after listening to the news? Or worse? Consider taking a break from it all.
- Email: go through your email and delete everything that's cluttering up your inbox. If there's a bunch of salesy newsletters you're tired of, unsubscribe.
- Turn off all website and app notifications on your browser and phone.

- Social media: You now have permission to unfollow, unfriend, or downright block negative people from your newsfeed and your life. If someone asks you why you're doing it, say it's a social experiment for a class.

I LOVE Facebook and use it regularly on a desktop, but I have a newsfeed blocker. If I want to see someone's posts, I have to go to their wall, or visit a shared group. It helps me feel more in control. I spend a lot of time socializing on Facebook, but I come away feeling good versus feeling overwhelmed. I don't have it on my phone because I want to limit the amount of time I'm distracted on the app.

I keep social media apps off my phone. Are there a few you could use a break from, that you could delete or log out of now? Free up time and mental space. Remember, the news and social media apps aren't free. You don't pay money, but you pay with your time and attention. What if you took all that time and attention and focused on what you wanted instead?

As always, the goal is to feel as good as possible, as often as possible, and to let go of the old patterns that molded the old you, so you can embrace the new version of yourself you want to be.

STEP SIX: Clear the Clutter: Bills

ASK the Universe to transform your finances and make room for your riches. You'll get the nudge to open a new savings account, sign up for a budget making software or follow a FIRE (Financial Independence/Retire Early) finance blog. The Universe will send you a new tax person, or a way to save on your loan payments. Or you might be inspired to go through all your bank accounts, line by line, and cancel memberships and subscriptions that no longer bring you joy.

Negative feelings like guilt or shame might come up. Clear them away with this mantra: "I now clear away my feelings about my bills and bank account."

STEP SEVEN: Give yourself a hug, pat yourself, and go take a nap. The act of decluttering is powerful but can bring up a lot of gunky feelings. It's okay to go slowly and get help. Ask the Universe to assist you and make the process of creating your new, wealthy life easy and effortless. You deserve it.

For the rest of your life, you'll go through a cycle of decluttering and clearing out the old to make room for the new. It's a natural cycle. Every second, over one million of your cells die. Your body works to purge them and replace them with young, healthy ones. You're a brand new person approximately every ninety days. That's great news!

Sometimes, you don't choose what to declutter. Sometimes, you float to a higher plane of self worth, and the Universe decides to clean out the old gunk that you've accumulated–the stuff that's holding you back.

This happened to my friend. At the start of her thirties, she got out of a bad relationship and took some time to herself. After a year or so, she went on a beach vacation, met an awesome guy and started a fairy tale romance. She was so happy.

In the next three months, the rest of her life fell apart.

Her phone and her car died. Her housemate of three years picked a fight with her and her housing situation fell apart. On Christmas Eve, she was fired from the job she'd held for five years.

Phoneless, carless, homeless, jobless. Merry Christmas.

You'd think she'd insulted the Universe's mother for the way it was treating her. But when you look closely, you'll see what really happened.

My friend had moved onto a higher plane of self-worth, one where she loved herself more deeply and expected her life to be better. She's a Scorpio and prone to holding on to the past. So the Universe helped her and tugged all the old crap she'd been holding on to out of her death grip.

She got a newer, better car and a shiny new Iphone. She left her housemate on good terms and moved in with family for a few months. It was during Covid, and she could safely be in a bubble with her two-year-old niece and four-year-old nephew and didn't have to quarantine alone. Her family was grateful for the extra help and pair of hands with their littles, and it helped my friend to have a rent-free place to land.

As for her job, she'd hated it and wanted to quit for years. She had planned to quit that January but was hanging on to help out during the holiday. Her boss was unbearable and the job was crushing her sense of self-worth, but she felt loyal to the company. Even when she planned to quit, she probably would have probably told her boss to keep her number "just in case." Nope, the Universe wanted her to move on. A higher power cleaned out the clutter so my friend could move on to her new awesome, better life.

Within days of being fired, my friend got a new job where she can work her own hours from home and get paid over double what she made at her old crap job. She now lives in a gorgeous yellow six-bedroom Victorian home with her beau. He loves to travel and took her on a dream trip to Europe. She has plenty of time and money–a whole new wonderful life.

If you're in the middle of these Adventures and everything in your life starts leaving, breaking, blowing up or going wrong, don't despair! You're moving to a higher level. The old is falling away to make way for the new. Ask the Universe to make it easy and show you how much you're loved and cared for. Between you and the Universe, you'll declutter your life so there's space for all your dreams.

Bonus: Ask the Universe to help you declutter your life and make the process easy and magical. As the old falls away, revel in the freedom and spaciousness of your new life.

ADVENTURE FOUR

To forgive is to set a prisoner free and discover that the prisoner was you. –Lewis B. Smedes

Congratulations! You've spent the better part of a month exhuming your money blocks and setting them on fire. This week you're going to shed more mental and emotional burdens so you can make space for amazing riches to pour into your life.

Step One: Cut the cords

In August 2015, I sat down and made a list of people I could rely on. For years I'd been trying to make friends, but after all my effort to connect and support others, I only had acquaintances. When I wrote out the list, I included only people I felt gave equally to our relationship. If I invited them to go for coffee, they made an effort to show up. They supported my dreams. They encouraged me. I could count the number of my friends like that on one hand. But I was at peace. I wasn't going to chase anyone. Mentally, I released everyone else from friendship with me. I cleared out my energetic Rolodex™.

Later that month, I connected with an author online. She invited me to an author conference in Arlington, DC, a few hours from my home. I went and walked out of that conference with twenty new friends who were all published authors. One of those authors, Renee Rose, is my best friend. She's like a sister to me. We did so many marketing projects together, we started co-writing and then founded a publishing company together.

Take the plunge and release the cords binding you mentally, emotionally and spiritually to others.

To clear the energetic cords between you and others, follow the steps below, or use the cord clearing meditation available in the Money Magic course.

How to play:

Relax into a comfy position with some relaxing music playing, like the Reiki list on Spotify. Imagine one of your friends or family members in front of you, with a glowing gold thread connecting you to them. Sometimes the cord is thick like steel thread. Sometimes it's gossamer thin, no more substantial than a spiderweb.

PRETEND one end of the cord is velcroed to your heart space, and peel it away. Tug it off the other person, too. You can imagine cutting the cord between you first using scissors or a machete, but make sure you unhook the thread from both you and them so it doesn't re-form.

I SET a reminder in my calendar to do this meditation on the first of every month and clear the cords between me and the people closest to me in my life. I also repeat "I clear my relations with ___" about all my family members, even my children. I don't want to get stuck in old patterns of relating to my loved ones. They grow and change, and so do I, so I allow our relationship to grow along with us. I don't want to treat my six-year-old the same way I treated him as a baby.

THIS EXERCISE DOESN'T HARM you or the other person. Instead, it frees you both from an old pattern so you can reconnect on new, loving terms. Try it now!

STEP TWO: Make a list of all the people who've wronged you and forgive them. Say or write in your journal, "I now forgive ___ and release all unforgiveness I've been hanging onto."

. . .

IF YOU CAN'T FORGIVE them, ask the Universe to forgive them for you. "Please forgive ___ for me and release all unforgiveness from my soul and body."

REPEAT this over and over again until you feel light and free.

EARLY IN MY AUTHOR CAREER, I had to do this with a person I thought was my friend. She talked about me behind my back and convinced a group of friends that I wasn't to be trusted. But when I look back at the situation, I attracted a lot of it with my negative thoughts and behavior. She recently subpoenaed me in a lawsuit, but the situation ended up turning out in my favor. My lawyers handled the response—and didn't even charge me for their time! When I look back at how events turned out, my life is better because I left behind a group of negative people who weren't really my friends, and found a circle of amazing, positive people who lift me up.

IT TOOK a while to forgive her, but when I finally got sick of holding a grudge, I asked the Universe to forgive her for me. I instantly felt lighter, and I don't feel gross when I see her name come up anymore.

NOTE that I am no longer seeking her out as a friend. She betrayed my trust and I have no interest in interacting with her again. But that's okay. I'm not carrying around the burden of negative feelings about her anymore.

. . .

Take it a step further: think of the best possible thing that could happen to the people you need to forgive and wish that for them. This is so powerful. You immediately become bigger than the situation. So full of love and joy that all your hurts begin to heal.

One of the rules of the Universe is you reap what you sow. If you're planting seeds of anger and grudges, you're going to reap more situations that make you angry and inspire you to hold a grudge. On the flip side, any good thing you wish for another, you're actually wishing for yourself. Let Karma take care of avenging you, and sow only good things so you can reap the same.

Forgive people and wish them well. Lay down the burden of grudges and continue on your journey to wealth and abundance, lighter and freer than ever.

Step three: Forgive yourself.

Say or write in your journal, "I now forgive myself for any and every harm or hurt I've inflicted on myself. I release all grudges or unforgiveness towards myself. I understand that in the past, I was doing my best. I now clear all judgements and criticism of myself I've been holding onto. I clear my negative opinions and beliefs of myself."

. . .

Lately I've been dealing with writer's block. Over the years I've made a habit of holding tension in my body. This leads to pain in my hips and stiffness in my wrists. My body doesn't want to sit and write, and then I judge myself for being lazy, which leads to more resentment and a whole cauldron of anxiety. I've taken steps to live more abundantly and treat my body with respect–investing in yoga, physical therapy, Thai massage and other body work to unlock my hips and learn to work without holding tension. But the final step to healing is forgiving myself for all the years I forced my nose to the grindstone even though it was breaking my body. Forgiving myself for holding tension and stress. Forgiving myself for judging myself as lazy, even though I'm hard working and doing the best I can. I am clearing my blocks over and over, and releasing myself from all the angst of past writing sessions so I can float into my blissful and creative future.

So often we're weighed down by the criticisms and judgements we have of our bodies, our looks, our work, and our worth. This puts us at war with ourselves. We're our own worst enemy, and we know how to hit where it hurts. But it doesn't have to be this way. Clear your mental burdens and experience the renewing of your mind. Take a moment and forgive yourself now.

Step four: Choose to love yourself

"Love yourself first, and everything else falls in line." – Lucille Ball

. . .

IN THE HARSH, cold month of November, 2014, I was stuck in a sales job I hated. It was commission based, and I'd worked so hard for five years, only to burn out. In a month, I was turning thirty years old, and I felt like I'd wasted my twenties chasing after money with depressing results. I was broke and desperate, and worst of all, I'd denied myself my lifelong dream of becoming a writer. Why? Because I didn't think I could make any money as a writer. No one I knew earned a living telling stories, so I told myself it wasn't possible.

ON THE EVE of my birthday, I made a life-changing decision:
"I now love myself. I'm not waiting for the day I drink enough water, earn more money or lose ten pounds. Right the fuck now. And I'm not waiting until I'm eighty to pursue my dream of being an author. I'm not putting off my desire to create my art until after I've had babies and raised them, like Grandma Moses. I'm doing it now. I choose myself now."

IN JANUARY, 2015, I self-published my first fiction books and earned $50. I continued to build my author career, signing with a publisher and then choosing to indie publish a series I'd thought up in college. That series earned my first six figures. I got a job in financial sales to earn money, but it wasn't until I left that job and pursued my dream that I became wealthy beyond my wildest dreams.

. . .

It all stemmed from a decision to love myself unconditionally. It's time now to unleash the power of love into your life.

"I choose myself now."

You're almost to the end of the hardest leg of this journey. You've started to go on adventures with the Universe. You've practiced gratitude and love, and in doing so, felt feelings of joy. You've also dug into your negative beliefs and cleared out a bunch of clutter: mental, emotional, physical and spiritual. You've done such amazing work! It's only going to get more and more fun.

But first, you have a big decision to make. This decision will change your life. You'll make it over and over again, every time you decide to step up and have your own back. You've already made it in a lot of ways. Now it's time to really commit.

Decide, right now, to love yourself. Not when you lose ten pounds. Not when you drink more water. Not when you finish your degree or get your promotion or find true love. Right. Now.

Give unconditional love to yourself and watch yourself blossom. There are so many things, situations, and experiences waiting for you, but you have to allow yourself to want them. You have to believe you deserve them. I want this for

Adventures with the Universe

you more than anything, but only you can give yourself this gift.

Love yourself. Right now. No more waiting. It might feel scary. You might protest "but I'm not worthy! I need to earn my degree, get a job, qualify for a mortgage. I need to hit ___ milestone to prove I am loveable."

Bullshit. It's time to clear away the belief that you're not worthy, deserving, lovable just as you are.

Ask the Universe to help you love yourself. The Universe might guide you to go back to Adventure Three and clear out any physical clutter that's reinforcing your low self-esteem. Or harken back to Adventure Two and repeat "I now deeply love and accept myself, just as I am" and clear any negative echo that bubbles up. Take a shower and imagine all hatred and self-judgment washing down the drain. Or book a massage and get help releasing the 'issues in your tissues.'

Make a list in your journal of all the things you love about yourself. What do you love about your body? Your mind? Your face? Your life? Start with the easy answers, the features or quirks in your personality you're most proud of. As the week goes on, ask the Universe to show or remind you of your unique beauty, creativity, genius and most loveable bits.

Take a bath or lie down and get comfortable under a cozy blanket, and imagine the Universe blanketing you with love. Imagine it saturating every part of you. It doesn't matter if your hair is frizzy or your feet stink. You are loveable. You can also ask the Universe for help finding the best hair care products or a luxurious foot care kit–you deserve it!

In Month Two, you're going to go on four more Adventures that will lift you up and give you proof that you are worthy of love. But for this week, dwell on the feelings of love and forgiveness, and be gentle with yourself.

You are loveable. You are worthy. You are deserving of all the wealth and success you can imagine–and more!

MONTH TWO: BELIEVE

"Until we feel worthy—deep inside—of the great life we desire, we won't feel worthy of money on the outside."
—Nancy Level

The best part about being in a state of abundance is how joyful you feel—about money, about success, about the ability to receive the things you want, and watch your wildest dreams become real!

WITH THE NEXT FOUR ADVENTURES, you will practice feeling abundant. And you will amass concrete evidence that you are worthy of wealth beyond your wildest dreams. This proof will make a strong foundation for new, positive, and powerful beliefs.

ADVENTURE FIVE

"*Goals in writing are dreams with deadlines.*" - *Random Pinterest quote*

IN 2006, I went through a rough patch. I was a sophomore in college with a stressful course load, my parents were divorcing, and I gained a lot of weight. A lot of my beliefs about what life should be were shifting. I was in a Bible class at the time, and we made lists of our perfect partners. I took it seriously and wrote down a page of qualities I wanted. Things like "loves kids, good father, good person" along with "hot, billionaire." Okay, maybe I didn't take it too seriously. I tucked the list away and forgot about it.

Five years later, I was packing up to move in with my new husband and digging through an old box of memorabilia, and I found the list. I laughed as I read it, especially when I came to the "billionaire" part.

But when I got to the end of the list, I got chills. I'd written: "What exactly does he look like? Don't know, don't care. Maybe he has blue eyes and brown hair."

Reading those lines on my old want list freaked me out so much, I almost threw the sheet of paper across the room. It wasn't the fact I'd written the list. It wasn't reading silly things I'd written, like "billionaire."

The list freaked me out because I'd manifested it. Not the things I didn't want. But if I went down the list and circled the qualities I still wanted in a partner—swapping out "billionaire" for "well off and great with money"—it would describe my new husband perfectly.

I'd found that list in a box of old things because I was moving. I was moving because I'd met an awesome guy. He has brown hair and blue eyes. He's never been religious, but he and his parents are some of the most moral, best people I know. His whole family takes time to volunteer with the nonprofit First Robotics. He told me, early on, that he loves kids. Immediately I thought, "he'd be a great dad."

The first time I saw him, I wasn't impressed (and he didn't think much of me. According to him, I was wearing "an ugly Grandma sweater"). But we ended up hanging out more and talking and really hitting it off.

The first time we hung out one on one, we spent the entire day together. We met at the gym we both used and walked on treadmills next to each other for forty-five minutes, talking about our childhoods. We had so much in common. I invited him to go to Lewis Ginter, a local botanical garden. From there we went to Lavender Fields Farm, where we visited a cute little gardening shop and he bought fancy composting bins. Our date ended in his backyard where we set up the composting bins. He was so excited, and I remember thinking, "I have to marry this man. Who else would set up composting bins with me on a first date?"

. . .

In November 2013, I did.

It's time to make a list of everything you want to manifest! In Step One, you'll use your journal and brainstorm all the wonderful experiences, life-changing amounts of money and cool stuff you want to pull into your life.

Step One: For this first step, settle down with your Adventures with the Universe Journal and a nice new pen. Write out a list of what you want in this season of your life– an item, a job, an opportunity, an amount of money. Write it as you want to see it happen in your life.

Here's my current list:

- a lithe and healthy body that's strong enough to do lots of yoga handstands
- my kids to have world class teachers and an incredible education experience
- my business to earn 7 million this year
- a freshly renovated second floor of our house, with nice wood floors and beautiful rugs, new paint and decorations to make a cozy hygge space
- a fabulous trip to Tuscany where everything goes smoothly and I'm able to see lots of art and stunning sights, and eat lots of pasta and gelato. A trip of a lifetime!

Adventures with the Universe

. . .

HERE ARE A FEW IDEAS:

Clothes you want to wear
Foods you want to eat
Gorgeous and fun stuff you want to own
Items, big and small, you want to buy
Places you want to travel
People you want to meet
Experiences you want to have

WRITE as much or as little as you want. Be specific if you can, but if writing something vague like "I want a new car" because you're not sure if you want a Tesla Y or Tesla 3 and writing down "new car" makes you feel excited, keep it general.

IF YOU HAVE something specific in mind, let yourself write it down. Don't worry about whether you'll change your mind on having it later. If you do change your mind, the Universe will know. Remember my want list for a husband? I manifested the right man who fit what I truly wanted. Make your want list and don't worry whether you won't always want some of the things you write now. When the time is right, you'll manifest what you truly want. It'll be perfect. You are meant to experience life to the fullest. Your desires are sent to entice you to enjoy life in different ways.

. . .

If you need some inspiration, here are items I wanted that I've manifested:

- A writing career. I have old journals filled with affirmations like "I am a bestselling author." I find them and take pictures of the statement and post it in my Facebook groups where I hang out with all my author friends. I manifested this in 2015... although I didn't earn much money until 2017.
- Bestselling books. I have many books that have received a #1 Bestseller tag on Amazon. And books that have hit the USA Today Bestseller list. First time hitting the USA Today Bestseller list was in 2016 with a book in an anthology.
- Earn six figures. Manifested in 2017. I earned close to 150k of income from my novels. Combined hubby and I were earning six figures even when I only made 20k from my books.
- Earn seven figures from my books.
- A husband and cute, healthy kids. I got married in 2013. Bebe 1 came May 2016 and Bebe 2 came April 2018. And they are so cute.
- Healthy hips – I was in constant pain in 2020, and now I am pain free and growing stronger every day. Best of all, I take time to do yoga and treat myself. My life is more balanced.
- An awesome yoga studio
- A trip to Paris and awesome friends who invited us to stay in their gorgeous apartment in the Sixteenth Arrondissement, and also toured us

around the best local places to wine and dine and buy cheese and *pain au chocolat*.
- A trip to one of my favorite cities, Edinburgh, and the money to stay in the Caledonian in a room with a perfect view of the castle. Great weather to hike Arthur's Seat on a path lined with gorse in bloom.
- A white Tesla X bought at the end of 2017, and a new garage built in 2018. (In hindsight, I'd have waited to buy the brand new car until the garage was built. Our old garage was more of a shed and we didn't realize it wouldn't hold the Tesla.)
- A gorgeous writing space and Herman Miller Eames lounger to chillax in.

Whenever I get in a funk, I can look outside at the new garage that houses our Tesla and remember how I manifested these things. We all have tons of beautiful items and experiences we've manifested over the years. That's why we started this game with gratitude.

If you're having trouble getting started, try this version of the game:

The Complain Game

How to play:

· · ·

THINK of all the things you don't want. All the things you're complaining about. And then write out the opposite scenario of what you're hating. I jokingly call this the Complain Game, but it's really the Want Game turned upside down.

HERE'S an example from my journal in 2020:

- I want my hips to stop hurting. I don't know why they're hurting but I've ordered a new mattress pad and seat cushion to try. If that doesn't work, I'll get a new mattress and office chair. I also should probably do more yoga. Ack! Universe, fix this.

THIS COMPLAINT BECOMES...

- I want healthy hips that allow me to walk and sit and stand pain free.
- I want a comfortable bed that allows me to wake up refreshed and feeling great.
- I want an excellent place to sit to work. I love my writing business and I deserve the best chair and desk that support me while I let the words flow.
- I want a great yoga class with a kick ass teacher. I deserve to take the time to stretch my hard-working body. Even if my cat and kids drape

themselves all over me when I do Downward Facing Dog.
- I want a great schedule that allows me all the time I need to take care of my body. (I already have this. I've just needed to allow myself to take time off to go to yoga)
- PS. I'm so grateful for my body and my hips. I never think of all the ways we use our hips and how important hip flexors are. Most of my life they have worked pain free and I have taken them for granted, so I'm going to be super grateful for great hips now. Thank you, thank you, thank you.

HAVE FUN WITH THIS. Your goal is to end up with a big smile on your face and an excited feeling that good things are coming to you.

REREAD your list and imagine it all coming into your life until you feel giddy. How will you feel when all the things you want appear in your life like magic?

HERE ARE SOME EXAMPLES: Abundant, Free, Excited, Wonderful, Safe, Loved, Ecstatic, Powerful, Content, Supported, Magical, Victorious

WRITE out the feelings in your Adventures with the Universe Journal, and dwell on them. Feel those feelings now. Intensify them until your body vibrates with the giddy sensation. Pump your fist into the air. Get up and dance!

THEN, let your Want List go. Just like in the Magic Spell you completed in Adventure One, fold up your new extended Want List and put it into your "Ask the Universe" box. Once it's in there, you've surrendered it over to the Universe. Your only job is to listen and follow any nudges the Universe gives you to move towards your goal.

Step 2: Window shopping

"Life is an endless unfolding." - John Gardner

YOU'VE STARTED your Want List, but the truth is you'll always have one, and you'll always add to it. Every time you see an experience or gift you want for yourself, whether it's a happy couple smooching in the airport or a fancy latte, you are subconsciously adding to your Want List.

THIS WEEK, as you go about your day, your world is the Universe's magical department store, a menu of delights you get to order from. You can order as much or as little as you like. Every time you see something you want, tell yourself "I can afford that."

Adventures with the Universe

. . .

Go for a walk past your favorite stores. Every time you see something you want, say "I can afford that!"

Online, browse your favorite shopping websites and put items on your wishlist or in your cart.

Go to realtor open houses or car lots. And tell yourself:

>I can afford that!

>I can afford that!

>I can afford that!

My favorite way to play this game is to go to a real estate website, click through beautiful beach homes, and affirm "I can afford that" each time. It doesn't matter whether you're looking at nice pens that cost a few dollars or million dollar mansions, your goal is to say "I can afford that" as many times today as possible.

. . .

You don't have to say it out loud. Thinking it in your head is enough. But when you say, "I can afford that,", if you hear a negative echo pop up—"No, you can't! What are you crazy? You can't afford that, not if you worked a million years!"—the second part of this step is to clear that rebuttal away. "I now clear my feelings and beliefs about money."

I can afford that!

<negative echo> "No, I can't."

"I now clear my feelings and beliefs about money."

Keep it light, and keep it moving. Today is all about fun. When you find things that you're super excited to buy one day, tell yourself "I can afford it" over and over. Do it until you have a big smile on your face. Revel in that feeling!

Step 3: "I'll have some of that please!"

This step will align you even faster with the life you want. Let me first explain the concept behind it.

. . .

HUMANS ARE SOCIAL CREATURES. We're not wired to achieve *something*; we're wired to become *someone*. The fastest way to change your habits is to surround yourself with people who are already practicing the habits you want. For example, if I wanted to start running marathons, the first thing I'd do is find and join a group of people who run marathons. It might take years or only a few months, but pretty soon I'd be buying the same running shorts as my new friends, chatting about how to avoid shin splints, and meeting them in my favorite park for a run.

I KNOW THIS WORKS, because I've done it over and over. Not only with hobbies, but with career changes, too. The best thing I did when I decided to be an author was join a Facebook group for writers. I noticed an author in the group who wrote books for a publisher I'd been researching. The author, Bella, had a Union Jack flag as her profile picture. I messaged her letting her know I saw her in the women's writer's group and wanted to write for her publisher, but also admired her avatar because I'd studied abroad in London. She replied that she'd lived in England, and now lived in Richmond, Va, like me. Did I want to connect?

OF COURSE! I replied. She suggested a coffeeshop in Church Hill, and I agreed. "I love that place. I live up the road."
"Really? Where?" Bella asked.
"On O street."
Turns out Bella lived on O street too. When we met, she invited me to a conference hosted by her publisher–the very publisher I wanted to write for. I walked out of that conference with a publishing contract in the bag.

. . .

THE FASTEST WAY for you to become abundant is for you to align yourself with people living in abundance. Unfortunately, you might have practiced resistance towards people who are wealthy and successful. That was true for me. My mom always told me "Rich people are evil. Rich people are selfish and greedy." And it was true for her—--she met and worked for people who happened to be rich, mean and selfish. I had to clear this belief.

THE FUNNY THING IS, once I cleared it, I started noticing how many people who had money were also kind, awesome and generous. Not that they were perfect. No one's perfect.

PERSONALLY, now that I practice abundance and have all my needs met and plenty of money, I find it easy to be generous and give more of my time, love and money away. I'm not perfect, but life is a lot more fun, and I think I am able to give more now that I have more.

SO TODAY you're going to start to align with people living in abundance. Whenever you see someone who has the life you want, you're going to bless and praise them. I learned this from a teacher called T. Harv. Eker in his Millionaire Mindset book.

HOW TO PLAY:

. . .

Adventures with the Universe

WHENEVER YOU SEE someone go by in an electric Porsche Taycan in the exact sky blue color you want, bless and praise them. Whenever you see someone enjoying success you'd love to have, bless and praise them. Say: "I bless and praise you." If you don't like the word "bless" you can say "affirm" instead. You don't have to say it to them, just say it under your breath:

>I bless and praise you.

>I bless and praise you.

>I bless and praise you.

AND THEN TELL THE UNIVERSE, "I'll have some of that, please!"

>I'll have some of that, please!

>I'll have some of that, please!

I'll have some of that, please!

IMAGINE the same wonderful things you're witnessing happening to you. If any negative feelings bubble up, clear them away. Feelings of jealousy push abundance away. Why? Because when you're jealous of someone, you're silently affirming two subconscious thoughts:

1. I want what they have
2. I don't believe I can have it

I THINK you'll notice that #2 is a money block! If you desire it, you can have it. It might not show up in your life exactly the same as it does in another person's life, but it can show up as the highest and best version for you.

NOTICE who you're jealous of and why. Affirm to yourself "I'll have what they're having." And then tell yourself, "I deserve to have it." If you hear a negative echo, clear it away!

YOU'LL FIND that jealousy and envy is a great way to discover what you want and uncover the abundance block that's keeping you from it. When you find yourself turning into a green-eyed monster, tell yourself "I can have that too."

. . .

GREAT NEWS: whatever good things you're seeing, you're starting to attract into your life. You're on the right track. The Universe is showing you different items on the abundance menu and asking you if you want to manifest those good things in your life. Don't push away the things you want with jealousy. Bless and praise the people who have them and say, "I'll have some of that, please!"

ADVENTURE SIX

"Dream boards provide a visual of the energy I'm pulling in for my future. They keep it right in front of me so I can dip in throughout the day and indulge in the sensation of what I'm calling into being." -Renee Rose, author of Write To Riches

You spent Adventure Five compiling a physical and mental list of the things you want.

Time to take it a step further and surround yourself with the images of what you want! The simple act of writing down what you want can powerfully attract it. But we're also visual creatures, and pictures speak to the deepest parts of our mind. This adventure is a fun way to stay focused on what you want, especially if the pictures inspire happy feelings.

One of my friends does dream boards every year. In 2022, she put up a picture of the USA today bestseller list with a note that her goal was to have a bestselling book land on the list five times. When she was redoing the board for 2023, she realized she'd done just that.

Other friends have manifested new cars, vacations, career awards, and even a new baby.

I asked a few friends for their dream board stories, and one author named Trudi gave me her story. She was part of a mastermind where she wrote out twenty-one pages of goals.

"AT THE TIME, reading 21 pages felt a little too overwhelming (surprise, surprise), and I didn't think I was getting the right vibe, so I decided to do the same thing in pictures. But again, because I was in over-achiever mode, instead of doing a one page dream board, I did a dream BOOK, so I could look through the book, and get the feeling for each goal I was aiming for.

Somehow looking at pictures of each of the things I wanted made it more real for me, and made it so I could feel the feelings of actually achieving the things I wanted to achieve. For most things I had a couple of pages of images and words that felt right for me."

SHE THEN GAVE me a huge list of what she had manifested from her dream book, including:

- A new mountain holiday home – bought in July 2022.
- A new red car with the license plate WRiTER – bought it in September 2022 for her birthday.
- Ski trips.

- More adventures, including a helicopter ride up the Tasman glacier, a boat cruise over a glacier lake, zip lining, white water rafting (twice), roller blading, eating lunch with keas (alpine parrot), went zorbing (rolling down a hill in a huge ball), jet boating (multiple times all around NZ), and even a freefall experience.
- Losing 10 kg (about 22 lbs).
- Grading up to a red belt in karate—*"This was a funny one. I tried so hard in 2021 to make this happen, I was all focused on that red belt but because I was focused on getting the belt, it stopped being fun, and I started missing classes, and then we had lockdowns, so I missed even more classes. Then at the end of the year, when I didn't get to go to a grading, I was gutted, and decided to flag the whole red belt goal and go back to just enjoying going each week. I just made it my goal to not miss a class... and lo and behold, my sensei said in about March 2022 that he wanted to put me forward for my red belt. It felt like I just relaxed and then suddenly things happened. I didn't do the grading for a couple of months, and I ended up getting a whole bunch of one-on-one sessions with my sensei which helped with my fitness and my confidence, and by end of May 2022, I had graded up to red belt. It was like I relaxed my chokehold grip on the end goal and just let it happen, and everything fell into place."*
- Turning her home into a haven – adding a walk-in wardrobe in her bedroom, a pool in her backyard, a new office and a new kitchen.
- Hiring a housekeeper and a gardener.

. . .

Let Trudi's story inspire you to get creative!

Step One: Create a dream board

Grab a bunch of old magazines or turn on your computer printer. Ideally you would be able to create a physical dream board for you to hang on your fridge or over your desk. But collecting images digitally can work too, so start a new file on your computer or new Pinterest board.

Invite the Universe to guide you, and send you art or images that represent what you want. Follow the nudges.

Gather pictures that inspire you. Cut pictures and words out of magazines and pin them to your dream board. If the images are digital, save the files somewhere you can easily find them. I have a Google document labeled "Dream Board." Pinterest boards, a file on your phone or desktop–anything can work.

Here's what I have on my current Dream Board:

- A picture of muscadine grapes growing on a trellis to inspire my gardening.
- A picture of a woman's beautiful smile, because I want brilliant, healthy, white teeth.
- A picture of a light-filled bathroom I downloaded as inspiration for my own bathroom remodel—

(the bathroom is done so you could say I already manifested it).
- A few pictures of bikini clad yogis doing handstands on the beach, to inspire my yoga practice.
- A picture of Marigot Bay, a beautiful resort in St. Lucia, where I want to hold abundance retreats.
- A picture of an electric jet, from the POV of someone enjoying the flight.
- A picture of my book on an airport bookshelf. (I put it there to take a picture, but one day I will see my books sold in airports all over the world.)

HAVE FUN WITH THIS. The goal is to play and feel good. If any negative feelings bubble up, clear them. Don't get bogged down worrying how all of this will manifest. Everything you want wants you. Ask the Universe to send it to you. Continue to clear your money blocks and dwell in a state of gratitude, and what you want will manifest in your life so fast, you'll be in awe.

ADVENTURE SEVEN

"The sky is not the limit. Your mind is." -- Another Pinterest quote attributed to both Lynette Simone and Marilyn Monroe

In this adventure, you're going to get really specific about how to manifest more money into your life and bank account. Do this adventure and you get comfortable having large amounts of money in your life. You will normalize wealth. When more money comes into your life, it won't trigger your money blocks and make you freak out. You'll relax and receive.

WHEN MY SON was about to start kindergarten, my husband and I took him to the school playground to play on the swing set. We went to the school open house, walked the halls, toured the library and met my son's new teacher and some of his classmates. We told him, "You're going to have so much fun going to kindergarten."

We took the time to normalize the new experience. And on the first day of school, he strode right into the building and gave his new teacher a hug.

Our brain's top goal is to keep us alive. Not happy or rich, just breathing. Our mind loves the familiar, because it recognizes it. If -$106 in your bank account is normal, then your brain is happy. But if you expand your comfort zone so $106,000 in your checking is business as usual, then your brain will allow that sum into your life without panicking and sabotaging (or spending it all away).

New things are scary! Fantastic news, there are things you have or do now with joy and ease that used to be new and scary. Like tying your shoe or going to first grade. Or driving a car.

My mother taught me to drive. Who thought it was a good idea for humans to hurtle down an on ramp at forty-five miles an hour, and zip into place with other vehicles zooming past at sixty-five miles an hour? I left permanent fingermarks on the steering wheel during the "merging onto the highway" driving lesson.

As I held my breath and prayed for the other drivers to let me into the right lane, my mom told me, "One day, you'll do this without thinking."

I was gritting my teeth too hard to argue with her, but I knew there was no way merging would require less than a white-knuckle grip on the steering wheel and lots of prayer.

Three months later, as I guided the giant blue boat of our family's minivan onto the highway to flow with the other cars, I remembered what my mother said. She was right. What I struggled to learn was now a habit. I merged into traffic, and all I was thinking about was how well my voice blended with NSYNC's as I sang along to the radio.

Is there anything you do today that you were petrified to

try only a few months, years, or decades ago? Write them down as part of today's gratitude list in your Adventures with the Universe Journal. And then complete the following steps to build belief that being a millionaire will one day be as easy as kindergarten.

STEP 1: Create Your Dream Bank Account

I WROTE myself a check for ten million dollars for acting services rendered and...I dated it Thanksgiving 1995... just before Thanksgiving 1995, I found out I was going to make ten million dollars... for Dumb and Dumber. – Jim Carrey, Oprah Winfrey Show, 1997

ONE OF THE reasons I have my Dream Board mostly in a Google doc is because right at the top, I have an image of the bank account I want. In this step, you're going to make an image of your dream bank account and keep it somewhere special, either in a secret Google doc or tucked into your journal, or, if you're comfortable, tacked to a corkboard over your desk for all to see. Normalize seeing wealth in your bank account!

HOW TO PLAY:

GRAB A BANK STATEMENT, either a physical print out or digital one. I've done both.

If it's a sheet of paper, cross or white out the total and

put in the new total. (I learned this from *The Secret* movie). If it's digital, figure out how to make a copy and alter the image. Or cut/paste the data into a Word doc, delete and type in the new numbers (this is what I did).

Example:

Bank Account #XXXX
    Available Balance: $105,136.01

Put in any numbers you want! Put in different numbers and play with it. I tend to put random looking numbers in. Imagine if your bank account really did have this amount. How does it feel? Tap into that feeling.

The goal isn't the amount of money, it's the feeling. So play with the numbers but don't forget to practice that abundant feeling.

I did this a few times with my monthly statements. I'd go down the list of deductions and turn the minus (-) signs into plus (+) signs. I'd imagine all that money flowing out of my account to pay bills was really getting deposited into my account. Then I'd add a few zeros and commas to the balances. If my husband found these altered bank statements lying around, he probably thought I was crazy. But I seriously practiced feeling what it would be like to have $36,000.00 in my checking account. And you know what? Now I have that money.

. . .

Do this for your investment accounts also. If you don't have a retirement account, I recommend you open one. Put in the minimum amount required to open it, then print out the statement and put in whatever total you want. Pause and imagine what it would be like to have that amount of money. Do any money blocks pop up?

Recently I typed "9,000,000,000" into my money tracker and immediately heard the negative echo "I don't deserve that." This is an awesome way to uncover your money blocks.

Whenever those negative beliefs and feelings come up, clear them.

A note on negative feelings: you might have had that money once and now it's gone, and now you have a huge money block. You might have strong feelings of anger and sadness and shame because you "lost" money. You might believe that if money comes into your life again, you'll lose it again. And you've decided the pain of losing money isn't worth it, so you're blocking money from coming to you in the first place. Which has its own set of problems.

Or maybe you never had money, but you've watched others earn it and lose it, and you've decided money equals suffering. The result is you're suffering anyway.

First, thank the feelings. Be grateful for your money blocks. They're trying to protect you.

Once you've acknowledged your money blocks and thanked them, play with the idea of letting them go. You don't need protection from money. Money isn't good or bad, it's just money. It can be destructive or a useful tool, just like a hammer. A hammer isn't good or bad, it's just a hammer.

Money is meant to flow in and out of your life. Remember, the word "currency" comes from the same root as "current," meaning "in circulation." Money isn't meant to stay in your life and stagnate. The richest people don't hide their money in a jar in the ground. They invest it and send it out into the world to reproduce. That act of releasing it actually allows in more and more money—the same way planting seeds instead of eating them allows you to reap a harvest.

We're challenging some deep-seated beliefs, so be gentle with yourself. If these adventures are too intense, ask the Universe to help you. You might get the nudge to go back and play some of your old favorites again. Repeat the Magic Spell in Adventure One and practice dwelling in love and gratitude. You'll tip the balance of your feelings to mostly good, and then you can come back and try these more advanced Adventures.

Step Two: Abundance Tracker

I tend to be less organized around money. My husband does our taxes, manages our business payroll and makes sure there's enough in our personal checking to keep the lights on. But I took an awesome course by Denise Duffield-Thomas and took her advice to start tracking my income. Taking time to record all the credits hitting my bank account gives me millions of opportunities to feel grateful. Since I started keeping track of all the dollars and cents that flow to me, my income from my werewolf romance novels has grown year over year, from around $150,000 in 2017 to over a million a year today.

How to play:

. . .

Download this abundance tracker or create one for yourself. In a separate journal or program like Excel or Google Sheets, label sections for each month. You're going to record every time money comes into your life. You can track salaries, royalties, the $5 slipped to you by grandma in your birthday card (I get these even though I'm in my thirties). Go through all your bank accounts and record all the times money hit your account. I include everything from the fifty-six thousand that came in from Amazon from my werewolf romance novels, and the 30 cents my bank gave me in interest. I didn't include my husband's salary when he was working for G.E. because I just wanted to track the money I was responsible for, but if your partner's money enriches your life, feel free to include it!

Definitely include inheritances, gifts, money won, money earned, interest earned—(this gets a little complicated with my investments, so I tend to ignore those accounts). I coached one author whose goal was to earn six figures a year. Turns out she already was earning close to that—but she wasn't counting her income from Apple Books, Kobo, or Barnes and Noble. If your goal is to embrace an abundance mindset, don't discount any money. It all counts. (I'm preaching to myself. Maybe I will include my investment money, but track it on a yearly basis).

Set aside time weekly to track your money. Or, if you're super stoked about this step, daily. I like to write the date and the source of the money.

You can also track the value you manifest. For example, to support my back, I bought a Herman Miller Aeron chair. But instead of buying it new for $1,100, I checked Craigslist. A man was selling a few of his old office chairs for $345. I'm sitting on the chair now and it's working great. The difference between the full price and the price I paid is the value I manifested. When you take the time to record all the value you've been given, your eyes will be opened to the abundance you're already swimming in. Plus, it's another chance to be grateful!

Think back over your entire life, and write down all the value you've received. All the meals you ate your caretakers provided. All the gifts. All the oxygen you breathe and water you drink. All the beauty you've enjoyed for free.

You're surrounded by abundance. You have been all along.

Whenever you pay full price for something, you can practice gratitude. "I'm grateful for the money to pay this bill." Whether you revel in paying full price or finding a great deal, you can feel abundant.

If any negative feelings come up, clear them. "I clear my relationship with money." Focus on feeling grateful for what you do have. This is the most important part of this step. Look over all the money coming into your life and feel grateful. Even if it's only a few pennies. What you're grateful for, you'll receive more of. So be grateful for the pennies and they'll grow into dollars.

STEP THREE: Create Your Dream Bills

IN THIS STEP, you're going to attract your dream bills. No, that's not an oxymoron.

Think I'm crazy when I tell you paying bills can be fun? What if the Universe handed you ten or a hundred times the amount you needed to pay each bill, and you could keep the rest? And the money you sent out went to good people who are working hard to feed their families—and you felt awesome about paying them because they provided you with tons of value? How would paying bills feel then?

I've gotten to the point where paying bills feels amazing. For example, when this book is done, I'll send it to my editor, Sharon. She's awesome and her input will make this book better. When she's done, she'll bill me $575 and I will happily pay it. She's given me so much value and I feel grateful to know her.

Once the book is edited, I'll send the final draft to my audio producer, Stephen at Vitruvian. He has a studio in Brooklyn, and he'll hire a voice actress to narrate my books. With the money he charges me, he'll pay the actress, cover rent at his studio, upkeep his equipment, and use the rest to go to a pizzeria and tip the waitress.

And maybe, just maybe, that waitress might buy this book. Which allows me to pay my bills and starts the cycle all over again.

See how much fun it can be to pay bills? I've got a big smile on my face imagining Sharon and Stephen and an actress and a waitress all moving through life, gaining and spending money. It helps that I have plenty of money to spend. But I got into this abundant position by feeling grateful and good about money, even when my bank account was in the negative and I could never have imagined paying hundreds or thousands of dollars out of pocket to anyone.

There was a time when paying my bills gave me chest pains. If it's been the same for you, let's try this game.

How to play:

. . .

GRAB YOUR BILLS. Write out the amounts in your journal. Then, beside it, write a much, much larger amount. I typically add a zero. If your bill is $300, write $3,000 beside it. Now imagine the Universe handing you $3,000. Imagine paying your bill and having plenty of extra money left over. Feel grateful for the money.

When negative feelings come up, relax. Feeling bad about bills is super common. Clear these blocks to get some fast relief.

> "I clear my beliefs about my bank account."
> "I clear my beliefs about my checkbook."
> "I clear my beliefs about my debt."
> "I clear my beliefs about bills."

AFTER YOU'VE CLEARED, write out all the reasons you're grateful for the bill. Can you feel grateful for your electric and water bill? What about your grocery bill? The honeycrisp apples you bought for snacks, the new Lisa Kleypas romance novel you grabbed in paperback, the hand sanitizer that smells like lavender? What about toilet paper? Can you think of a few reasons to be grateful for toilet paper and all the good it brings into your life (and how grateful there's plenty available in stock)?

For every bill you pay, focus on the value you received. Imagine the money you're paying blessing the people receiving it.

. . .

Adventures with the Universe

NOW REPEAT THIS AFFIRMATION:

Every dollar I spend comes back to me one hundred fold.

IMAGINE if every dollar you spent returned to you with ninety-nine of its best buddies. How awesome would that feel? Feel into this feeling. Every time you pay a bill, repeat this affirmation and imagine ten times the amount flying into your bank account immediately.

Another way to play: grab an old bill or statement. Cross out the total and put a smaller total. Or put $0.00. Or the words "Paid in Full." I did this with our mortgage statement a few times. Last fall, we paid off our mortgage completely! With cash! (Note: Mortgages can be awesome and useful. You can keep them and still feel abundant. But it is fun for us right now to own our home free and clear.)

This Adventure can be challenging. If it's no fun right now, set it aside. Go back to Adventure One and repeat steps one and two. Get back into a good feeling state. You can come back to this Adventure when you feel like it—or skip it and move on.

There are many ways to clear your money blocks and move you into abundance. If one adventure makes you feel sick to your stomach, forget it and focus on the ones that make you feel good now.

The goal is to feel good and love yourself.

ADVENTURE EIGHT

"My tastes are simple, I am easily satisfied with the best." - Winston Churchill

In 2021, I earned over one million dollars from my fiction books. I'd always dreamed of being an author and making a living writing books. Now I was making a fortune–earning seven figures in a single year. But I didn't feel any different. I didn't feel any more excited or abundant, even though I'd hit a huge milestone.

While journaling one morning, the Universe helped me realize two things:

1. I set big goals, like earning a million a year or hitting a bestseller list, because I thought that by achieving those goals, I'd be worthy. Worthy of celebration. Worthy of more love, more adoration, more praise.

2. I didn't have to wait for anyone else to celebrate me. I don't need a trophy or a marching band. I can celebrate myself.

Can you spot the money block in number one? We don't have to achieve anything to be worthy of love, adoration or praise. We deserve those things as we are.

The second realization knocked me out of my Aeron chair. When I picked myself up off the floor, I copied out my realizations onto a notecard that I stuck into the cork board above my desk. Then I asked the Universe to help me celebrate my success in a way worthy of a millionaire author.

A few weeks later, I followed the nudge and bought a pair of hoop earrings studded with lab grown diamonds. I call them my millionaire earrings, because whenever I wear them, I feel like a millionaire.

In this Adventure, it's time to celebrate yourself, because you are worthy now.

Step One: Tiny Upgrades

Take $10-20 and go buy some small items that will make your life instantly better. Here are some ideas of what to buy:

- New pens: I'm a writer, and there's nothing worse than grabbing a pen to jot down a grocery list, only to have the ink sputter and die in the middle of the word "lettuce". Now I buy awesome new pens that I love. Basic ink pens, not pens that can

write in space or underwater or anything like that. Nice pens that work don't cost much money and they make me so happy.
- Music: I used to cut my budget down to the bone, leaving no room for fun stuff. When I finally decided to splurge and buy a monthly subscription to Spotify, I felt so wealthy! I upgraded to the family option and gave away memberships to my family.
- A nice pillow. You can never have too many cute pillows.
- Treat yourself to coffee, lunch, or a small dessert. Or buy a nicer brand of coffee or tea and a beautiful mug—these are other writer essentials.
- A new toothbrush: You probably have a new one in a drawer under your bathroom sink. You just were holding off using it.

IN ADVENTURE THREE, you let yourself get rid of the old, grungy, or useless items first. One of the reasons we hold onto old stuff is because we're telling ourselves: "I can't afford it. I better stick with the old, because if I let it go now, I might need it later, and I might not have any money in the future to buy what I need. Plus, I don't want to waste money on myself. I don't deserve nice things."

When you take this step, the underlying message is "I am worth nice things. I trust I will have the money to buy what I need in the future." So subtle, but it sends a powerful message to the Universe.

The moment you buy the item, affirm over and over: "I can afford it! I can afford it!" Remember, as you buy and use and enjoy the new small item, you are living in abundance. Feel the good feelings as intensely as possible for a minute or two, then get on with your day.

Go splurge on something wonderful that costs under twenty dollars. If anyone questions why you're doing it, you can say "I have to for a class."

Step Two: Lifestyle Upgrades 2.0

You've spent weeks going on adventures with the Universe and clearing out your abundance blocks. It's time to splurge! You're going to spend money today intentionally, as part of your lifelong destiny to let your surroundings reflect your new abundant state.

How to play:

Take $20-100 and invest in an upgrade to your life. Here are some ideas:

- Upgrade your bath mats and shower curtain.
- Buy pretty pottery mugs. Coffee/tea mugs are an essential part of this writer's ensemble. I also buy really excellent coffee and tea.
- Go out to lunch or dinner by yourself or with a loved one. I am a big fan of treating myself to dinner. You can still go on dream dates if you're single—take yourself!

- Treat yourself to a movie out.
- Splurge on a car wash.
- Hire someone to mow your lawn or complete a small chore you've been putting off.
- Buy yourself nice new pillows and sheets. Or towels. And a silk pillowcase!
- Upgrade your phone charger.
- Decorate with a new plant.
- Buy yourself fresh flowers.

THE GOAL IS every time you use your new mug or sheets, or see your nice shiny car or fresh flowers, you feel abundant. You feel like a million bucks. You're living in luxury, one small step at a time. Feel the good feelings. Feel amazing and tell yourself you'll always have the money to treat yourself to what you want.

If any negative feelings arise, clear them. And ask the Universe to help you. The other day in the shower, I realized I had a huge block when it came to renovating and updating my home. Whenever I felt the urge to plan for a new kitchen countertop or full bathroom remodel, I told myself, "No! Renovating is exhausting. Loud, noisy, dirty and expensive." It's no wonder I didn't want to do it! As I stood under the warm water, I cleared that block, and asked the Universe to make renovating easy and fun.

Within a few hours, I was creating Pinterest boards labeled "upstairs renovation" and "downstairs bathroom" and pinning all the lovely, hygge things I could find. I even pinged my friend for ideas, and she sent back a bunch of texts with advice, followed by "I'd love to help you create your dream home."

A week later, on a walk with my husband, I brought up our monthly budget and all the projects we wanted to accomplish in the year. "We can do the power wall for the solar roof first, and then update the garage the way we want." Our garage has an upper room we plan to turn into an office/meeting space with soft gray walls, pale oak floors, a Murphy bed for guests, and a private bath.

"Or we pull the trigger on both," he replied. "We have the money to do it all now." He ended up doing all the work to interview and hire the contractor, and when he dropped off the deposit, the contractor told him, "We can start tomorrow. But after your job, I'm booked up for months. You got in the queue just in time!" They finished insulating and mudding the walls in less than a week. Next is painting and installing the (heated!) wood floors. And I haven't had to lift a finger.

Invite the Universe to help you upgrade every area of your life, and look for the good that follows. You might get a gift of money or the exact item you wanted. Or a clear download that helps you picture the romantic gold and white decor you love, plus a coupon to a tile store and the burst of energy (or a best friend) to help you create the bedroom of your dreams.

As you upgrade areas of your life, you affirm to yourself that you are worthy of your dream life now. Best of all, you are living it! And that is abundance.

MONTH THREE: ALLOW

"You can do some rather extraordinary things if that's what you really believe." - Toni Morrison

In this month you're going to expand your feelings of self-worth even more, so you can enlarge your capacity to receive. Then you can sit back and let the money flow to you.

ADVENTURE NINE

"You are the master of your destiny. You can influence, direct and control your own environment. You can make your life what you want it to be." Napoleon Hill, Think and Grow Rich

You may have heard of Napoleon Hill's "Think and Grow Rich." Now it's time to "Nap and Grow Rich." I'm serious! I used to think I was the world's laziest meditator, but every time I wake up from my "meditation nap" I feel refreshed, relaxed, but also like my brain shifted from first gear to fifth. I'm able to go faster with more ease.

Meditation is a powerful way to knock out your money blocks. In November of 2014, I went to a hypnotherapist, hoping he'd help me remove whatever was stopping me from earning six figures in my financial sales job. It worked—too well. After one session, I left energized to focus on my dream of being a writer. By January, I had self-published several novels I'd written, and started to earn money as an author. By August, I'd quit my sales job and signed with a publisher.

Then I met my friend Renee Rose, and she regularly uses meditations to clear her negative beliefs and invite money to flow to her like magic. Together, we wrote a bestselling book series. We called it our Million Dollar series long before it had made a million dollars. Now our books earn over a million a year! Renee and I love believing big and focusing on abundance so much, we bake it into our days and we have a monthly membership called Money Magic where we encourage other business owners, authors and creators to do the same!

Step 1: Nap and grow rich

How to play:

Sit or lie down and get super comfortable. You can download a meditation app or find a guided meditation in our Money Magic course. You can try hypnotherapy–my favorite online teacher is Marisa Peer. You can also check out the free meditations on my Youtube Channel. Or simply play relaxing music and let yourself zone out. Mentally run down the items on your want list. Imagine they've already manifested. And feel grateful for them. Focus on those good feelings and amplify them as much as possible.

Another visualization I use comes from *Feel Free to Prosper* by Marilyn Jenett. She encourages you to close your eyes and imagine money raining into your life. Imagine it piling up all around you. You only have to reach out and pick some up.

You can also listen to this audio I designed to help you relax and focus on abundance. Don't worry if you fall asleep. I usually do. It works anyway.

Step Two: Affirmations

Once you're done napping, build on the great momentum by repeating positive statements to yourself during the day. But beware! Most people are doing affirmations wrong.

Remember the negative echo? Every time you say a positive affirmation you don't believe, like "I deserve to be rich." --the negative echo kicks in and resists the positive affirmation.

When you say the affirmation "I deserve to be rich", resistance kicks in and you think these thoughts: "No, I don't. I don't deserve to be rich. I can't even balance my checkbook properly. And who wants to be rich? Gross. Rich people are mean. I don't want to be rich. If I'm rich, people will judge me."

Before I figured out the negative echo, every time I said a positive affirmation, I was really affirming something else. I could affirm "I am rich" all I wanted, and it would never manifest, because I didn't believe it. My feelings were all focused around my real affirmation "I don't deserve to be rich. Being rich is bad." The real affirmations were the ones I believed, the ones that inspired strong feelings. My affirmations were working. But they were the wrong ones.

This is the main problem with affirmations. If every time you try an affirmation "I deserve to be rich" your follow-up thoughts and feelings affirm the opposite, you're pushing on the accelerator while jacking up the emergency brake and your car is going nowhere.

But the good news is this: you're already using affirmations and they're working. Now we have to figure out ways to make you believe the affirmations that will get you the results you want.

The first affirmation you'll try is a simple one from a great book I read by Marilyn Jenett called *Feel Free to Prosper*. She encourages using affirmations but points out a lot of us have mental blocks to statements we don't really believe are true. This is a problem because when we're broke and trapped in a scarcity mindset, we tend to believe the negative affirmations we use like: "I'm broke. I'm always broke. I'll always be broke." Those thoughts make us disbelieve the positive affirmations that would pull us out of our scarcity rut into abundance: "I love money. I'm attracting abundance. I deserve wealth."

Even if you still have some money blocks to clear, Marilyn Jenett is a genius and came up with a statement that shouldn't trigger your brain's cascade of negative thoughts and feelings around money.

How to play:

Repeat the words "Wealth and success" silently or out loud. Allow the pleasant images those two words conjure up to float around in your head.

Try it now:

> Wealth and success.
> Wealth and success.
> Wealth and success.

Do this several times today. Your brain will focus on whatever you tell it to, so over time this statement can be very powerful. Start to notice the examples of wealth and success the Universe puts in front of you. And then you can say "I'll have some of that, please!"

Step Three: MOAR Affirmations

People will say affirmations don't work. This is because they haven't cleared their nasty, negative beliefs, so every time they affirm something positive, the negative echo kicks in. If your negative feelings are stronger than your high frequency feelings, you'll remain stuck in scarcity. Affirmations work, but make sure you're affirming the right thing.

Great news, saying the following affirmations is a great way to flush out your money blocks. When you hear the negative echo, you've got a golden opportunity to clear it away.

How to play:

Repeat the following affirmations. If you hear a negative echo, say "I now clear my beliefs about money."

I now clear my beliefs about money.

I'm surrounded by wealth and success.
I am open to receiving abundance.
I am meant to enjoy life.
I am worthy.
I love abundance.
Abundance is all around.
I am open to living in abundance.
Abundance is pouring into my life now.
My life is full of wealth and success.
I am gratefully receiving abundance.
I enjoy life.
I am living my best life now.
I am worthy.
I am living in abundance.
I am wealthy.
I love money.
I have so much money.
Money pours into my life easily.
I have all the money I need.
I am so grateful for all the money I am receiving.
I love being wealthy.
I love earning money.
I easily earn money.

People give me things all the time.
I am open to receiving all good things.
I love having money.
I love saving money.
I love investing money.
I love organizing my money.
I am a brilliant money manager.
I have so much money.
I always have the money I need.
Money comes to me easily and effortlessly.
I am so grateful for my wealth.
I am so grateful for my life.
I am living in abundance.
Everyone and everything prospers me now!

I recorded an affirmation audio you can access on YouTube. Feel free to record your own voice saying these audios and play it on loop.

ADVENTURE TEN

"Educate yourself, make your world view bigger, visualize wealth, and put yourself in the picture." -KRS-One

In this final month of adventures, our focus is "acting as if" you already have the abundance you desire. You've spent time focusing on what you want and reducing your resistance to it. It's time to let the Universe do its part and bring what you want to you. Your only job now is to focus on feeling good—getting on that high frequency that allows Abundance to flow into your life.

MY HOPE IS you'll be able to access that high frequency and feeling state any time you want. For me, positive books and audios help me focus on the beautiful truths in life.

STEP 1: Become a Scholar of abundance

. . .

How to play:

Go to the library or splurge and buy some of the following books. I prefer books on audio because I listen to them when I'm in the car. Here are some of my favorites:

- *The Secret* and *The Power* by Rhonda Byrne
- *Beyond Positive Thinking* by Dr. Robert Anthony
- *Ask and it is Given* by Abraham Hicks
- *You are A Badass* by Jen Sincero
- *The Success Principles* by Jack Canfield
- *Get Rich, Lucky Bitch* by Denise Duffield-Thomas
- *We Should all be Millionaires* by Rachel Rodgers
- *Write to Riches* by Renee Rose

There are tons of different teachers, each with a different style. Explore and find whatever flavor of "self help" you like. You want to find and plug into anything that gets your head in an "anything's possible" space. Fill your days with positive texts and audios and feel into the lovely, happy feelings.

I've gotten to the point where I just get in the car and I access those happy feelings—because I've practiced listening to *The Power* or *You are A Badass* over and over and over.

Feels good, right? That's what you're looking for. Pure, happy feelings untainted by any negative emotion. Enjoy the positive, clear the negative. This is the frequency of abundance.

STEP 2: Find your Models

I LEARNED the concept of modeling from Anthony Robbins. I mentioned earlier that humans are social creatures and we become like the people we surround ourselves with. The great news is that these mentors and models never need to know our name. I've gained so much wisdom from Rhonda Byrne and Jen Sincero, and we've never met. But their words have changed my life.

You already went on an Adventure where you bless and praise people living the lives you want. Now it's time to find the people who are living the exact life you want, and focus on them.

HOW TO PLAY:

FIND the people who are crushing it in the areas you want success. People who are living a life you'd love to live.

WHAT YOU FOCUS ON EXPANDS. So focus on the good things and the things you really, really want. Don't focus on what you don't want. If you're driving a car down the road, and you stare at a ditch, how long will it take for you to end up in the ditch?

. . .

Let's focus on what we want.

Here are some examples:

- I'm an author, so I look at authors like Stephen King and James Patterson, but also indie authors who write romance and the type of books I want to write. I read their books, I sign up to their mailing lists, I follow them on Facebook. I watch their videos on YouTube (if they have any). I buy their courses. I don't follow all their advice, but I implement what makes the most sense to me. I joined writer groups on Facebook and read all the posts and paid attention to the people who had the success I wanted. It works! I'm still doing this!
- If you want to be a surfer, find the best surfers. Follow them on Instagram. Start planning how you're going to visit or move to the beach. Study their career trajectory and see how you can emulate it in your own life. Figure out how you could move closer to where the action is—so you can be around surfers 24/7.
- If you want to be a mommy blogger, study your favorite mommy blogs. Sign up to their mailing lists. Take their courses. Read their books. Figure out how they run their blog and emulate it. Use the same website designer, blog style, etc. Try it and see what works. Ditch what doesn't work but keep trying.

- If you want to have beautiful abs, find a fitness guru with the abs you want and follow their program.
- If you want a gorgeous, remodeled home, buy a few home design magazines and gather ideas. Follow your favorite designers on Pinterest and sign up to their blogs. Make a list of exactly what you want to buy and ask the Universe to send you the money or the exact items, or something even better. Declutter your home and give away items to make space for the new ones.
- If you want great investments, study the top investors. Follow their advice.

STEP THREE: Find Your Tribe

WE BECOME like the people we surround ourselves with. It's great to find mentors you watch from afar. Take it a step further and completely surround yourself with people working towards the goals you want.

HOW TO PLAY:

FIND a community to support your new lifestyle. If you want to be a writer, join a writing group on Facebook. If you want to hike more, join a hiking Meetup.com group. If you want to be better at budgeting, find a free Facebook group and connect with people focused on the same goal.

. . .

If you want to surround yourself with people focusing on abundance, I recommend joining the Money Magic course. I run it with my good friend and co-author, Renee Rose. Together we teach you more ways to clear your abundance blocks–and we have regular live calls you can join where we use our spiritual gifts to energetically clear the group's abundance blocks. With the course, you get access to a community where we record our manifesting successes and root for each other!

ADVENTURE ELEVEN

"Whatever a man sows, that he will also reap." - Paul the Apostle, letter to the Galatians

This game will align you with abundance super-fast. Remember, what you give, you receive. I learned this game from a book called *Happy Money* by Laina Buenostar.

STEP ONE: Give money

HOW TO PLAY:

TODAY, find ways to give a little extra money.

. . .

WAYS TO GIVE MONEY:

- Tip extravagantly.
- Leave a $5 or $10 bill with a post-it note that says something like: "This money is for you. I've found giving money away makes me happy. Please take this cash and allow it to bless your life." I left a $20 bill with a note like this in a little free library—lying in front of the books so it was easy to see.
- Send money anonymously to someone in need.
- Donate money to your favorite charity.

GIVE WITH A GLAD HEART. Imagine the money going out and blessing the people who receive it. Imagine it transforming their lives in a huge way and feel happy for them. Feel excited and happy about money.

THIS GAME SMASHES the belief "rich people are evil" to smithereens. You're proving to yourself that if you have tons of money, you'd be able to give more. You'd be able to bless the world in so many extra ways. Who better to be wealthy than you?

STEP TWO: Give Value

. . .

Adventures with the Universe

WHATEVER YOU SOW, you reap. If you sow seeds of scarcity, you reap more fear and greed and experiences that make you feel lack. If you sow seeds of abundance, you reap a life filled with wealth, confidence and success.

TODAY YOU'RE GOING to give value to the world. When you give with a glad heart, you absolutely must reap back good things. It's a law of the Universe.

HOW TO PLAY:

TODAY, focus on giving extra value. Here are some examples:

- If you are an author or creator, give something you made away. (As an author, I give away a lot of free books.)
- If you're an employee, give extra—go above and beyond your job description today.
- If you're a stay-at-home parent, plan something special for your kids, like a scavenger hunt or a favorite meal.
- Pick flowers and arrange them into a beautiful display.
- Call a friend and sing them a song to cheer them up.
- Lend a helping hand.
- Write one thank you note—or several!
- Give kindness, give compliments, give love, give your time. And feel good.

. . .

THIS WORKS IN AMAZING WAYS, especially if you give value without worrying what you'll receive in return.

In March 2020, the world was shutting down. I felt so helpless. I'm not a doctor or a nurse, but I wanted to help. I got the nudge to do a big sale on the eight books in my top selling series. I called my co-writer and told her, "Let's give our books away."

"Great," she said. "I can make book one free."

"No," I said. "Let's make eight books free."

My husband had just quit his job and was feeling stressed about money. "I might as well get a job if you're going to give all your books away for free," he told me. But I was undeterred. This blockbuster sale felt right. I wanted to give something that could make the world a better place. I wasn't a doctor or a nurse, but I was an author and I could give the joy of reading an excellent werewolf romance novel to the world.

My co-writer and I ran the sale and ended up giving away over a hundred and fifty thousand ebooks as a special gift to people in quarantine. We gave away an entire series— it was free on Amazon for five days. She called me a few weeks later to let me know our sales on that series had more than quadrupled for the month! And the series continued to sell well year over year.

Tell the Universe you want to give your gifts to the world, and ask for a nudge in the right direction. Give from a place of generosity and joy. Don't give begrudgingly. If all you can give is a smile, that counts! Give good things to the world and you can expect good things in return.

ADVENTURE TWELVE

"Everything that happens to you is a reflection of what you believe about yourself. We cannot outperform our level of self-esteem. We cannot draw to ourselves more than we think we are worth." — Iyanla Vanzant

After my daughter was born, I went through a period of sickness and exhaustion. With my first child, I took time to go to yoga and nourish myself with green smoothies and Buddha bowls. But with bebe 2.0 came morning sickness. My book income was climbing, but my body was breaking down. In the months after the birth, I struggled to nurse my baby and keep running my business treadmill.

I wanted to reach my goal of a million a year. I'd blown past previous goals of six figures, quarter of a million and half a million, but in my exhaustion I couldn't see the way to a million a year. How would I work two to ten times harder? I was already running on empty.

I made myself stick to a grueling writing and publishing schedule, but I grew sicker and sicker. My children were in daycare, and I contracted every bug and virus they brought home. At one point I had a sinus infection, an ear infection and a virus that closed up my throat. These were illnesses my adult immune system should've been able to fight, but with two kids in diapers, I was struggling to get a full night's sleep.

That spring, I said enough. I told my co-writers I needed a break, and asked the Universe to help me run my business and make it easy. I declared March the "month of me" and cleared my schedule of everything but rest, relaxation and routines of self-care. I went to the doctor and got the medicine I needed. I bought and ate nourishing soups, salads and coconut yogurt, and scheduled regular time to have lunch out with friends. I signed up to different yoga and Pilates classes, and revisited the ones I liked. I enjoyed my month so much I repeated it in April and May.

Meanwhile, magically things happened in my business. I had an old dark romance trilogy, some of the first books I'd written. I'd self-published it early in my career, but I didn't like the covers or the branding, so I unpublished it. On a whim, I asked my friend Stasia Black to read the books and help me rework them. I expected her to tell me they weren't fixable. Instead, she ended up rewriting them–mostly book one, which I'd written in college. We found the perfect cover artist and relaunched the books together as co-written works. We both went all in on the marketing, and I ended having the most successful launch of my career. We made half a million dollars in a few months. My husband was so impressed he asked me to write more mafia romance!

Turning things over to the Universe and taking time to rest led to this breakthrough.

Even if you're making money, you might not be living in a state of abundance. When you're feeling abundant, you're relaxed and letting things flow to you. You take time to nourish yourself and your spirit. When you're running the treadmill of stress, you're re-affirming the belief that life has to be a struggle and earning money is hard. The irony is, if you took time off to take a nap, things might click and abundance might start flowing to you faster than if you pack your schedule with meetings.

This adventure is about taking the time to enjoy your abundant life NOW. You're going to take a vacation day and do all the things you'd do if you were ultra-wealthy. The goal is to feel baller.

Step One: Millionaire Day

How to play:

Plan a "Millionaire Day." What would your life be like if you had earned a million dollars last year, and were guaranteed to earn a million this year and for the rest of your life? Write out your perfect day. Then, take a day off and indulge in a "staycation." Live into your perfect day as much as possible.

Here's my Millionaire Day:

- I wake up whenever I want. Make tea with a beautiful tea pot and my fancy Earl Grey—the nice, loose-leaf kind.
- I settle into my favorite chair and write for a few hours
- At noon, I head to yoga in buttery soft yoga pants and
- I might stop into some cute shops and buy a gift for my friend before meeting her for lunch. I'll pay for our salad and sandwiches and tip extra!
- In the afternoon, I'll get a massage, then take a walk in a beautiful park. On the way home, I'll

>   buy flowers. At home, I'll put the bouquet in a
>   vase, then light a candle and relax.

This is my Millionaire Day. It's pretty basic, but when I do those things, I feel so wealthy and good. I am working on incorporating those feelings into my ordinary day.

You might plan a Millionaire Travel Day instead. I did that in January with my friends. We went to the Marriott Bonvoy Beach Club in Rio Grande, Puerto Rico. Visited the spa, hung out by the pool, walked the beach.

Your perfect day might include camping and hiking in the wilderness. Or drinking coffee in a Parisian cafe before buying the perfect scarf at Hermès. Or scuba diving off a coral reef in Australia or racing a Porsche Taycan around a track in Nürburgring.

Or you do the staycation version, and simply buy the best coffee for your French press and take a day off to lounge around in a bathrobe. It doesn't have to be fancy. The goal is to *feel* wealthy now.

Every moment you can, be still and feel into the fact that this is your life now. Practice being wealthy. Feel the feelings of having your dream life *now*.

ADVENTURE THIRTEEN

"Love transforms us. The deeper the love, the deeper the transformation." Laura Livia Grigore

If money was a person, what would your relationship look like? Is it your enemy? Your friend?

How have you been treating your friend "Money"? Do you push it away? Invite it in? Go hot and cold on it? Do you cuss it out when you pay bills but beg and plead for more time with it when it's payday?

Do you make space for money in your life? Is there room in your home, your wallet, your bank account, your investments for more? Do you like having money around, chillin' in your accounts? Do you thank money when it helps you do or buy stuff?

How could you be nicer to money? How can you encourage it to work harder for you?

This final adventure, you're going to woo money. Don't worry, it's easy. Money wants to be with you. It wants to engage. Currency is meant to flow like a current, and money wants nothing more than to flow into your life and be treated well.

If you feel judged or rejected by money, that's a money block. Go ahead and clear it and you'll feel how friendly and happy money is, and how much it wants to connect with you.

STEP ONE: Play the Gratitude Game with money. Write out all the ways you've had abundance in your lifetime. Go back to your childhood and list all the ways money showed up for you, even if you weren't aware of money's role in your life. Let's acknowledge the ways our parents and caretakers provided for us. They bought clothes, food, gas, and even spent money and time buying gifts for us.

- Did you ever take a vacation?
- Did you have clothes, shoes or a winter coat?
- Did you have food?
- Did you have time to play? Friends to play with? Toys?
- Did a teacher ever throw a party for your class?
- Did you ever get an award, a plaque or a medal?
- Did you ever get a gift?
- Did you ever get a ride to school or to a playdate with friends?

WHILE WE'RE AT IT, let's be grateful for the abundance the Earth gives us:

- Did you ever enjoy a blue sky? A rainstorm? A snow day? A beach day?
- Did you ever sit under a tree and find relief in the shade?
- Did you ever cuddle a pet? Or watch a bird splash in a puddle?

CHRONICLE all the ways abundance and money showed up in your life, without you even realizing it. Every sip of water you took, every cut that healed, every molecule of oxygen: take a moment to be grateful for it all.

How have you been treating your friend "Money"?

Step Two: Write a letter to money. Apologize for the cruel ways you've treated it or pushed it out of your life. Ask it to flow into your life. Outline the ways you're going to make space for it. Ask it to stick around in your bank accounts and invite more of its friends to party!

Put the letter in your Ask box or fold it up and burn it. Release your relationship to the Universe.

STEP THREE: Go on a date with money. Take a walk and point out all the things money can buy. Acknowledge all the free oxygen and sunlight you enjoy. Revisit the "Wealth and Success" affirmation outlined in Step Two of Adventure Nine. Repeat a mini portion of your "Millionaire Day" and dwell on how money makes it possible. Every time you make a purchase, thank the money you spend and invite it to visit you again. Ask the Universe to teach you more ways to love money and make space for it.

STEP FOUR: (Optional) Print out a picture of a hottie and write "The Universe is My Sugar Daddy." Place it in your purse, wallet or make like a '90s kid and hang it up as a poster over your bed.

CONGRATULATIONS!

"*Follow your bliss and the Universe will open doors where there were only walls.*" -Joseph Campbell

CONGRATULATIONS! You've made it through ninety days. I hope you've gotten in the habit of journaling and asking the Universe to show you your next steps. The adventures in this book were designed to build the habit of relaxing and turning things over to a higher power. Great news: you'll be on this Adventure for the rest of your life.

My non-fiction book coach, Lisa Daily, says "We write the book we need to read." While writing this book, I got to take a good, hard look at my year. Turns out, I'd built up a money block and wallowed in scarcity thinking for most of the year. I'd set an intention of taking the summer and December off, but was afraid my income would drop because I wasn't working hard enough. I spent the time I took off feeling grouchy and worried. And, yep, my income did drop.

I dug a bit further and realized a mantra I was telling myself. For two years I've been the sole angel investor in my husband's software-as-a-service (SaaS) startup. In SaaS terms, the amount of capital I'd invest was nothing. But to me it was a lot of money! And part of me resented "losing" it. My husband's company has incredible potential. Best of all, it's a tax write off. I'd either invest in him or spend the same amount in taxes. But I was repeating a negative belief over and over to myself: if I make more, I'll just have to give it to Justin. What's the point of earning more money…I'll just get bigger bills!

Every time I thought of making more money, I repeated this belief to myself. Affirmations work! Instead of making more money, my income stalled out and started to drop.

In late November 2022, in the process of working on this book, I uncovered this money block. Once I recognized it, I cleared it. I now affirm: "The more money, I make, the more I have. Yes, I'll invest it with my husband. But I'll also spend more on myself and my family, and save more for the future. As my income balloons, my expenses get smaller and smaller." This affirmation makes me feel AMAZING. Even if it has no effect on my bottom line, it instantly makes me less grouchy.

But it had immediate effects. In December 2022, my income zoomed upwards. Remember the Magic Spell in Adventure One? I've been practicing it over and over, and it's bringing breakthrough results. I finished out 2022 at $950,000 of income, and way more profit than I'd had in previous years. Turns out I was doing some accounting incorrectly, and had earned more than I'd realized. Best of all, I cleared a big fat money block and the future feels bright and sparkly.

Now it's your turn. What Adventure will you go on next?

Will you repeat the Magic Spell? Do you have more money blocks to clear? They can pop up even at high levels of income.

Read on for the FAQ and troubleshooting guide that might help you.

FREQUENTLY ASKED QUESTIONS & TROUBLESHOOTING GUIDE

Whether you think you can, or you think you can't – you're right." -Henry Ford

Help, I've tried all this before and it's not working!
Take a deep breath. Every second, you're growing and changing, remember? What was true in the past doesn't need to predict your future.

Let's shift your stuck feelings fast: Sit down and write out a list of all you're grateful for. Once you've written it, really dwell on the feelings of gratitude. This trains your brain to look for proof of abundance.

I trained my body to feel happy while sitting in traffic. In 2018-2019, my husband and I were working from home, but our littles were in daycare across town. Worst of all, they were in two separate daycares. With traffic, we had a forty minute commute, twice a day. It was a pain.

Driving down the highway one afternoon, I found myself bubbling over with joy. It was late fall and the way orange leaves popped against the blue sky was stunning. I felt lucky to be out and about on such a gorgeous day. I realized I felt this way every time I hit this stretch of the highway. Why?

Simple. I practiced those feelings. Every weekday on my commute, I listened to positive audiobooks. Books like: *You are a Badass* by Jen Sincero, *The Power* by Rhonda Byrne, *Feel Free to Prosper* by Marilyn Jenett, and *Ask and it is Given* by Abraham Hicks. I turned them on as soon as I left home, and by the time I hit that stretch of I-64, I was rejoicing. The sky wasn't any brighter than usual. I just noticed it. Despite my exhaustion from nursing two kids and working extra hours to build a successful business, my body learned to feel happy.

You can do the same. Play audiobooks on your commute. Put on uplifting music and dance around the house. Write in your gratitude journal on the bus. Train your chemical pathways to reach for good feelings–and ask the Universe to help make it easy and fun.

These grateful feelings can compound over time. Once you're in a good place, ask the Universe to shift your focus from the obstacle to the path beyond it. You might find the obstacle dissolves naturally. Or you'll get a nudge on how to jump over it. Ask the Universe to make it super clear what steps you need to take so you can move forward and create real change.

I DON'T KNOW *what to manifest/ I'm afraid to ask for what I really want.*

When we tell ourselves "I don't know" we're suppressing the intuition inside us that *does* know. Usually this is because we're afraid. It's okay to be afraid. Fear is trying to protect us. Over time you can build your trust muscle so when it's time for a leap of faith, you're able to let go.

Clear the fear. Take a shower and repeat "I now clear my fear about manifesting what I want." Imagine your fear washing down the drain.

Make a list of the times you felt afraid but you took a step forward and it turned out GREAT. This proof will build your belief muscle.

Repeat the "Wealth and Success" affirmation outlined in Step Two of Adventure nine. And when you declutter the digital clutter in Step Five of Week Three, unsubscribe from negative news sources, but subscribe to positive ones that fill your feed with proof of people succeeding.

When it's time to ask for what you want, start with something small. Do the Magic Spell in Adventure One, and when it comes time to make a list of what you want, ask for something small. Something believable. Often, we can manifest a good thing quickly when we think it's achievable.

Our brains can't distinguish between imaginary or real play. Play abundance games in your mind and pretend you know what you want. If you had $10,000 magically deposited in your account every day, what would you spend it on? Go make a dream board based on this make-believe money.

Start by dreaming. You see it in your mind first, and then the Universe will guide you to take the steps to make it happen. It works, whether you want a mansion or a cup of coffee. If it's easier to believe you can get the latte, start with that.

"If you have built castles in the air, your work need not be lost; that is where they should be. Now put foundations under them." –Henry David Thoreau.

. . .

WHAT IF I accidentally manifest something I don't want?

Newsflash: you have already. If you've dreaded an overdraft fee and watched it appear, congratulations! You've successfully manifested something. Now go focus on what you DO want.

If you stall on making a "Want List" because you might fill it with things you won't want in the future, don't worry. Remember how I made a list of attributes for my future husband, and then, when he appeared, he was the perfect match to what my present self would want? The Universe offers you an infinite amount of choices. Do you want the chicken or the steak? Neither? How about sushi? You get to choose. And you get to make new choices whenever you desire. So chose something that sounds good. Exercising your choices is a vote of confidence in the Abundant Universe. You're reinforcing that you know you can always change your mind, and the Universe will support you.

I KEEP TRYING to clear my money blocks and it's not working. I'm still broke.

Been there! It took a lot of clearing to remove my money blocks. Meanwhile, I cleared my blocks against going towards my dream career of being an author in an afternoon.

To relieve the stress, make a big list of what you're grateful for. Practice feeling grateful and happy–even for the things going wrong in your life. Remember what happened to my friend who lost her job on Christmas Eve? The Universe might be clearing away nasty old jobs, cars, phones, friends and homes to make room for the golden life you deserve. Trust that things will be better than before. Look for the moon in the darkest night.

This will start the shift. Simply saying "I clear this" can powerfully clear lots of abundance blocks, but if you need some extra help, there are lots of ways to clear your abundance blocks. I like The Sedona Method (you can google a simple article that outlines the process), the Cord Clearing Method, and tapping on acupressure points to rewire old patterns. I've also tried reiki, hypnotherapy, yoga, and meditation of all sorts.

You can also sign up to the Money Magic course I run with my friend Renee Rose. The course is full of meditations that help people shift their thinking, and each month there's a live call where we use our gifts to energetically clear everyone.

I CAN MANIFEST MORE MONEY, but then I sabotage myself. / I'm in a feast or famine cycle.

Good news, you've experienced the feast! You're halfway there. (How's that for cup-half-full thinking?) Whenever my money is low for the month, I practice feeling grateful for the better months. How would I feel like my money is low unless I'd experienced a new high? When you're in a down cycle, focus on gratitude for all the good that *has* come to you. You can spend your life looking for problems and things to complain about. Or you can look for the silver lining. And remember, the sun is always shining above the clouds.

A famine time is great for practicing gratitude and ways to quickly shift your feelings. In time, you won't fear the time between feasts–because you know you control your mood. And you'll trust a feast is coming. If you have fear that it won't, then you have the perfect opportunity to clear it.

What are you telling yourself during these highs and lows? What do you tell yourself before you head into a period of famine? Do you think similar thoughts when you're headed into a feast? Look for patterns of belief.

Maybe before a famine you think: "No use earning more money, I'll just owe more on taxes. Easy come, easy go." These are money blocks, and now you've uncovered them, you can clear them. Then turn around and affirm the things you want to believe. "I easily earn money. I've had challenges but I can overcome them."

I'M A CONTROL FREAK. It's hard for me to let go and let the Universe work its magic.

Babe, I am with you. If I could find the control panel for the entire Universe, I'd spend my life sitting in front of it. But that's not my job. It's not yours either. You might have a history of white-knuckling your way through life. You might have had a rocky childhood, where you had to raise yourself. Rest assured that the Universe is the one to trust with your being. Ask the Universe to show you a small way to surrender. Maybe you ask for a parking spot. Maybe you put an overdue bill in your ask box and ask the Universe to take care of it. Light some incense or a candle, pull out your journal and chronicle all the ways the Universe has provided for you in the past. Don't struggle to make up the list–ask the Universe to bring all the beautiful memories to mind. You'll receive a joyful download of the many times the Universe came through to bless your life. Give yourself a hug, take a bath.

. . .

I'm afraid to trust the Universe. The last time I did, nothing happened or things went wrong.

This is the perfect opportunity to allow the Universe to prove how worthy you are of love. Ask for the Universe to reveal its benevolence to you in the next seven days. Ask for a clear sign.

Fill a few pages in your journal with a Love list: all the things in your life you love. Ask for more of them, and record when they show up in your life. Ask the Universe to open your eyes to all the ways it *has* shown up for you.

If you're brave, ask the Universe to make sense of all the crap you've gone through. Vent your frustrations and ask for help understanding. Set an intention to feel safe and held–and record the proof in your journal when it appears.

I don't feel worthy of the things I'm trying to manifest. How do I get past that?

We don't rise to the level we want, we fall to the level of what we're willing to accept. There's a backlash against the "toxic positivity" in the manifesting movement, because faking positive vibes really doesn't cut it. Remember the "negative echo"? You can be affirming "I am a success" while still believing you're an absolute failure. That's why it's important to clear your negative beliefs and money blocks.

Each Adventure is designed to raise your self-esteem and feelings of deservingness. In Adventure Two, you clear your abundance blocks, including the belief: "I'm not worthy."

In Adventure Nine, you learn to affirm, "I am worthy, I am deserving, I am enough."

Sometimes it's more subtle. When you declutter the broken toaster in your home, you affirm "I'm worthy of nice, working appliances." When you upgrade your wallet from a worn and tattered purse to a beautiful Coach one, you feel fancy. It reminds you of your wealthy aunt, the one who's generous and loves paying for dinner out, who sends $100 every Christmas and birthday. You subconsciously shift yourself into her tribe, the "wealthy & generous" club. When you celebrate your success with fresh flowers from the market, you tell yourself, "I deserve beauty and things I love. My life is good."

Look over your life and find the places where you DO feel worthy and allow yourself what you truly want. I find it easy to treat myself to a latte, but I stall for months or years when it's time to upgrade to a new laptop. Meanwhile my husband has no problem buying top-of-the-line equipment for himself, but he will wear ratty and torn clothes long past the point where it's cool or fun.

Ask the Universe to help you carry that self-love and confidence over into other areas of your life.

I'VE TRIED SO many times and failed. How do I keep the faith?

The easiest way to build faith is to surround yourself with proof of what's possible. You can start by seeking out a positive community. Join my Adventures with the Universe facebook group to find like-minded folk on their journey to manifesting their dream life.

For extra help, seek out a teacher, or an energy worker who can help clean off decades of crud. After an energetic clearing, I feel like the clouds have parted. I knew the sun was always shining, but I needed some extra help clearing the clouds away. That's why I run a monthly membership called Money Magic with my friend Renee Rose. She has amazing psychic gifts and together we provide live coaching to energetically clear member's abundance blocks.

I do want to note: if you suffer from clinical depression or mental illness, it's important to seek medical help. I'd give the same advice to someone with a broken leg. If you fractured your femur, making a gratitude list might help your mood a little, but for fuck's sake, get your leg set first. Severe depression and anxiety run in my family and we're pretty open about seeking treatment. We throw everything at it, from doctor's visits to acupuncture, breathwork, meditation, forest bathing, taking extra B vitamins, and therapy. Our ADHD can contribute to our mental imbalance, so we find treatments and routines to help turn our neurodivergence into a super power that energizes us and fills us with creativity.

I THINK I resolved all my money blocks. What now?

Congratulations! If you're already feeling happy and in the flow, go do the Magic Spell in Adventure One and pull in some fun things that you want. Manifesting should be easy, like ordering a latte. No stress or worry about whether or not you deserve it: you get out of your way and go for it.

But at every level of income, you'll uncover other ways your deeper money block/beliefs present themselves. Like I shared earlier, I might be earning a million a year, but I get grouchy and stuck. I'm always finding negative beliefs and money blocks I put in my own way, or ways that I am fighting for answers and struggling when I could relax and receive.

For example, in March 2022, I was fretting about a reader conference where I was scheduled to sign books. I had a sign and many copies of my bestselling series with

Renee Rose. But I felt like I wasn't doing enough to promote my other books. I didn't know where to start. *Universe, please fix it!* Within a week, another one of my cowriters, Tabitha, told me she was interested in signing at the conference. I got the nudge to email the conference organizer to see if Tabitha could attend. We received an answer in minutes: YES! Tabitha ended up at a table next to mine, and she promoted my other best-selling series. It was a quick, clear answer to a problem I felt stumped on. All it took was a request, and the solution swept in like magic.

If there's any area in your life where you're feeling grouchy, that's a sign that you're not trusting the Universe. Maybe it's a negative belief or an abundance block. Or maybe you simply need to take a step back, take a deep breath and ask the Universe to help you. Life can be easy!

THE GREATEST ADVENTURE

"Take the first step in faith. You don't have to see the whole staircase, just take the first step." Dr. Martin Luther King, Jr.

Whenever I write about abundance, I find more success blocks to clear, and more ways I can believe in myself and allow more money into my life. Writing this book was no different. While working on chapters three and four, I added "Make an abundance block quiz" to my to do list. My husband has a software startup, and he offered to task his lead developer with the job. I outlined the task and they promised to work on it, and that should've been that. I could've relaxed, continued to work on the book, and waited for them to present me with their solution.

Instead, I fretted. I worried. I nagged. I changed my mind and tried to do it myself, trying multiple quiz software programs until I gave up and hired a contractor on Upwork to do it. I spun my wheels, expending effort and trying to force the quiz to get done. It didn't speed up the progress, it just made me a basket case and annoyed everyone involved.

I know why I didn't just relax and receive what I asked for. Deep down, I have the belief that: "I have to work hard for money." For some reason, I don't feel worthy of success unless I'm stressed out, grinding my teeth to nubs, losing sleep and fighting for it. This money block manifests all the time, in different ways. It's the reason I delegated the quiz, but still felt like I needed to do it myself. It's the reason I pick up toys and wash the dishes in the sink before my house cleaner comes, and I feel mortified that she has to tidy such a messy house.

After multiple efforts: signing up and trailing five different software programs until we realized they couldn't do what we needed, I paid the Upwork contractor $500 for a half done quiz. I tried a few more options on my own and gave up again.

My husband rolled his eyes at my struggle. This whole time, his programmer David was working successfully on the project. "Just tell me what you want," my husband said. "I am working on it. Let me handle it!"

I let go, and David finished the quiz. It looked great, cost nothing but David's time, used no expensive software, and did what I wanted it to do.

I told this story to Lisa, the coach who helped me write this book, and she laughed. "The Universe tells us the same thing," she said.

"Just tell me what you want. I am working on it. Let me handle it!" - My husband, and also the Universe

Over the course of this book, you've gone on Adventures with the Universe. As you've uncovered your abundance blocks and cleared them, you've grown and expanded your sense of self-worth. You've created a mindset where you not only want more, but believe you deserve it. Once you do that, the Universe rushes in to give you what it's been waiting to hand you all along: a life of ease and joy full of moments that thrill and uplift you. The adventures are designed to give you a taste of your best life, so you crave and demand it.

But we all fall into old patterns and feelings of unworthiness. Instead of relaxing and pulling in what we want, we choose to struggle. We sit in a ditch spinning our wheels when we could walk across the tarmac and board a private jet that's waiting for us.

So I'm writing this to remind you that in every moment, you get the opportunity to choose again. Stop in the middle of your stress filled day, opt out of the Complain Game, and remember what you're grateful for. Remember the times things did work out. Dwell on the feeling of ease and ask the universe to help you exist in that magical state again. Imagine everything working out. Get in the habit of switching from despair to hope, and eventually the "everything's possible" mindset will be the norm for you.

I wrote this book to remind myself that this is an option. Instead of worrying about writer's block or ads or dips in my income, I can start my day with a Magic Spell and ask the universe to give me a great writing session, connect me with a great marketing manager, and pull in more income. I can record my income highs and feel grateful for them, and ask for "More, please." I can spend my days decluttering what doesn't serve me, setting new boundaries, and upgrading to the new, wonderful life I deserve. And you can do the same.

I hope this book helps you relax and receive the abundance you deserve. I hope you'll stop putting brakes on your own desires and start letting what you want appear in your life. There are always areas in your life where you already feel abundant and worthy and you allow yourself to have what you feel you deserve. Maybe you love lattes and you have nothing blocking you from treating yourself to them. Maybe your house has indoor plumbing, and you don't even think about it as a luxury. But there are other areas where you can open up and receive the highest and best you can imagine–or something even better. After you remove your money blocks and get out of your own way, choosing your dream life can be as easy as ordering a latte.

Stop Putting Brakes On Your Own Desires!

Your life can be an endless Adventure, full of joy and magic, with both wild, exhilarating moments that make you feel alive and quiet, comfortable ones that make you feel at home. You can have it all. Ask the Universe to deliver, and it will.

STAY IN TOUCH!

Find me in the Adventures with the Universe Facebook group. And I hope you'll join Renee and me in the Money Magic monthly membership.

FREE RESOURCES

- Free abundance blocks quiz: https://adventureswiththeUniverse.com/quiz/
- The Adventures with the Universe Facebook group
- My website: www.leesavino.com/adventures
- Free meditations on my Youtube Channel

Remember to take the abundance blocks quiz: https://adventureswiththeUniverse.com/quiz/. It's the first step to blasting through the negative beliefs that hold you back!

MORE RESOURCES

- The Adventures with the Universe Journal
- The Adventures with the Universe Course
- The Money Magic monthly membership

Recommended reading:

- *Write to Riches* by my author bestie, Renee Rose
- *The Secret* and *The Power* by Rhonda Byrne
- *Beyond Positive Thinking* by Dr. Robert Anthony
- *Ask and it is Given* by Abraham Hicks
- *You are A Badass* by Jen Sincero
- *The Success Principles* by Jack Canfield
- *Get Rich, Lucky Bitch* by Denise Duffield-Thomas
- *We Should all be Millionaires* by Rachel Rodgers

Gratitude studies (check out the excellent video "An Antidote to Satisfaction" by Kurzgesagt)

Wong Y J, et al. Does Gratitude Writing Improve the Mental Health of Psychotherapy Clients?

Bartlett M, Condon P, et al. Gratitude: prompting behaviors that build relationships

Yu H. Gao X, et al. Decomposing Gratitude: Representation and Integration of Cognitive Antecedents of Gratitude in the Brain

Lúzie Fofonka Cunha, et al. Positive Psychology and Gratitude Interventions: A Randomized Clinical Trial

Philip Watkins: Thieves of Thankfulness: Traits that inhibit gratitude

Philip Watkins: Grateful recounting enhances subjective well-being: The importance of grateful processing

P. Kini, et al. The effects of gratitude expression on neural activity

THE AUTHOR'S GRATITUDE LIST

A big thanks to all the members of the Money Magic course and all the students in all abundance courses I've ever run, and to all my coaching students, who taught me as much as I taught them.

To Sharon, who edited this book beautifully.

To my werewolf husband, thank you for organizing the garage renovation, buying me the Herman Miller Eames lounger, and sorting out the abundance quiz. And the million other things you do to make our lives together a dream.

To my family, who loves and supports me even when I'm grouchy. Give me five minutes to finish this section and I'll come down for dinner.

To Nanette, my fiction books' biggest fan. You are a gift! Thank you for supporting my writing career.

To Renee Rose, my spirit sister, thank you for always calling me to new heights of abundance. We are magic!

And to Lisa Daily, who coached me through this book and helped me infuse it with joy. You're the best.

COPYRIGHT

Text copyright © 2023 Silverwood Press, LLC
All Rights Reserved

No part of this book may be reproduced in any form or by any electronic or mechanical means including information storage and retrieval systems, without permission in writing from the author. The only exception is by a reviewer, who may quote short excerpts in a review.

Neither the publisher nor the author shall be held liable or responsible for any loss or damage allegedly arising from any suggestion or information contained in this book.

www.ingramcontent.com/pod-product-compliance
Lightning Source LLC
Chambersburg PA
CBHW071243070526
44583CB00017B/2309